TYPING MADE EASY

TYPING MADE EASY

Featuring the "See it, Say it, Strike it" method

Elza Dinwiddie-Boyd

A PERIGEE BOOK

TO HERB

Perigee Books
are published by
The Putnam Publishing Group
200 Madison Avenue
New York, NY 10016

Illustrations by Lisa Amoroso

Library of Congress Cataloging-in-Publication Data
  Dinwiddie, Elza Teresa.
      Typing made easy : featuring the "See it, say it, strike it"
  method/Elza Dinwiddie-Boyd.
      p.   cm.—(The Practical handbook series)
      1. Typewriting—Self-instruction. 2. Electronic data processing—
  Keyboarding—Self-instruction.   I. Title.
      Z49.D55   1991   90-47468 CIP
      652.3'024—dc20
  ISBN 0-399-51671-9
  Cover design by Isabella Fasciano
  Printed in the United States of America
    3 4 5 6 7 8 9 10

Acknowledgments

I am offering a very special thank-you to my friend and editor, Adrienne Ingrum, who over the years has allowed me several opportunities to express my desire to write books. I am grateful to Laura Shepherd for overseeing the book to its completion.

Thank you to Lisa Amoroso for her fine line drawings and to Lisa Ponak for the clever letterhead designs. A special thanks also goes to Edward M. Cody of the Detroit Board of Education for reading the manuscript.

My dear friend and agent, Marie Brown, of Marie Brown Associates Literary Services, deserves many thanks for her continued support of my efforts in the field.

I am never able to offer enough thanks to my darling parents who raised me to have the strength and courage to work against the odds and to keep trying for the best. And to my Aunt Elza, Uncle Caudillo, and Aunt Nita who were always there as surrogates. I also owe a very special thanks to Dr. Fred S. Cook, my senior advisor at Wayne State University, who raised the teaching of Business Education from a science to an art.

My partner, my husband, is so essential to this process. Herb, thank you for helping make this happen. Again, I just know I could not do it without you, despite your protest to the contrary.

I owe so much to my dear students, who over the years have been so loving, so patient, and so supportive of my efforts to help them realize their fullest potential. And finally thanks to my friends and colleagues at the College of New Rochelle New York Theological Seminary Campus for their encouragement and support. Thank you, Dee, Louis, Jan, Pat, Sinclair, and Sharwyn for being there.

Contents

PART ONE:

The Importance of Typewriting

There are few active people who will not need to use the basic typewriter keyboard at one time or another. Many jobs in large and small corporations require employees to record and retrieve information quickly via the electronic keyboard. College and university students find that to remain competitive they must employ computer software and word processing systems. Many high school students discover that retaining a competitive edge demands excellent keyboarding skills. This book will show you how to teach yourself to type (keyboard) in a few easy lessons. It will show you how to acquire and maintain this important twenty-first-century skill.

WHO THIS BOOK IS FOR

The method of learning to typewrite presented in *Typing Made Easy* is called "See It, Say It, Strike It." It is a self-teaching course for mastering typewriters and keyboards and is for any motivated individual who realizes the importance of keyboarding to job success and as a vital component of one's entire package of life skills.

THE FOUNDATION

The first step in this keyboarding program is to look at your goals, your reasons for wanting to learn to type. Your goals will define the time span in which you want to accomplish this work. You should decide upon a target completion date, just like you would face in a classroom. How many weeks do you want to give yourself to do this? With your target date in mind, decide how many hours per week you will need to accomplish that goal. For example, if you decide to practice two hours per day you can probably complete the program in ten days. If you choose to practice one and a half hours per day you can probably complete the program in two weeks. The program works best when these concerns are addressed at the outset. Do not wait until after you have completed several practice sessions to assess your goals. Always allocate enough practice time for each practice session.

Take these steps before starting the practice sessions:

- Be realistic about what you can do and then plan ahead.
- Study your calendar carefully over the period you have set aside to accomplish your typewriting goal. Make sure the time you have scheduled to learn how to typewrite is not in conflict with other tasks. For example, if you plan to practice between 7:00 and 9:00 A.M. six days a week, DO NOT SCHEDULE ANY OTHER AC-

TIVITY DURING YOUR PRACTICE TIME.

• Allow for flexibility by identifying alternate times to shift your practice when a session must be missed.

Careful planning sets the foundation for continuing evaluation. Between practice sessions take a few minutes to reflect on your goals and progress. Use this information to evaluate and adjust your plan accordingly. Perhaps even after careful planning you will need more practice time to meet your goals. In other words think your plan through carefully and realistically before its inception and consistently evaluate your progress. This process will help you succeed on schedule. Advance planning minimizes the impact of those inevitable interruptions of the best-laid plans.

After you have planned your calendar to accommodate your practice on the keyboard, identify a permanent place where you can set up your typewriter, word processor, or computer. Allow enough space to keep all of your supplies together. It is important to MAINTAIN A NEAT, WELL-ORGANIZED, PERMANENT WORK AREA. Make sure your chair is comfortable and the keyboard is within comfortable reach. Good lighting is also important.

If you are using a computer or word processor, you will need to position your screen so that you minimize the chances of glare. It is best to use a computer stand that allows you to place the keyboard at the recommended height with the monitor positioned directly above on a slightly recessed shelf elevated 8 to 10 inches. Place the monitor so that the screen is in easy view.

Throughout your attempt to acquire this highly valuable skill you must maintain a high level of commitment to practicing on schedule. Motivation will be a key determining factor in your achievement.

Avoid practicing more than two and a half hours per session. When you practice excessively in one session, you may become fatigued and begin to practice errors.

As you proceed, you will measure your progress according to guidelines set forth in the book. You may need to adjust your target completion and/or length of practice time according to your progress and goals. The instructions that follow are designed to set the tone of your practice sessions. You should reread and practice the tone-setting phase until it becomes a habit, an automatic, reflexive, and precise response to the initial keyboarding activities.

THINGS TO AVOID

From the beginning you should avoid looking at your fingers except when told to do so. The goal is to memorize the key locations on the keyboard through your fingers. This is not an intellectual activity as much as it is an instinctual one, an automatic reflex.

The best typists keep their eyes on the material they are inputting. In the beginning you will need to look at your fingers from time to time to ensure they are correctly placed on the home row. Counting from the top of your keyboard, the home row is the third row of keys; from the bottom, it is the second. It contains: a s d f g h j k l ;. It is called the home row because it is on this row that your fingertips rest when you are typewriting. You will see that the SEE IT, SAY IT, STRIKE IT method introduces you to the keyboard by asking you first to locate the new key position with your eyes while watching your finger flick the key several times to establish a visual image of the reach in your mind. But, when that is done, you are no longer permitted to look at the keyboard. THE CARDINAL RULE OF TYPEWRITING IS TO LEARN THE KEYBOARD WITH YOUR FINGERS, thus rarely looking at your keys. TYPEWRITING IS A REFLEXIVE ACTIVITY.

KNOW YOUR MACHINE

Become familiar with the parts of your machine. Review the manual which came with your typewriter, word processor, or computer and become familiar with its functioning.

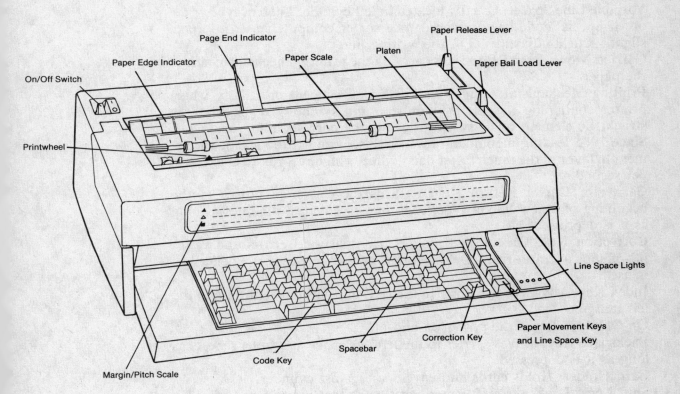

The Parts of a Typewriter and Their Functions

Cylinder: The roller around which the paper turns.
Cylinder Knobs: Located at each end of the cylinder; used to turn it. On the modern typewriter pictured above the cylinder is turned by a paper up and paper down code key.
Paper Guide: Guides and aligns the left edge of the paper as it is inserted around the cylinder into the typewriter.
Paper Bail: The bar with small rubber rollers that holds the paper against the cylinder.

Paper Guide Scale or Line Scale: Indicates the number of typing spaces on a given width of paper, shows the position of the paper, and serves as the scale for setting the paper guide.

Paper Release Lever: Used to straighten or remove paper.

Pitch Control: Switches the horizontal spacing between pica and elite typefaces.

Line Finder: Used to leave the original line of type temporarily to type a subscript or a superscript.

Line Space Selector: Controls the number of spaces (single, double, or triple) between lines.

Margin Stops: Used to set the right and left margins, the points at which the writing begins and ends.

Margin Release Key: Temporarily releases the margin.

Print-Point Indicator: Indicates the exact point at which the machine will print. On a word processor or computer this point is called the cursor.

Variable Line Spacer: Usually located in left cylinder knob of typewriter or via special code key on word processor or computer; used to make slight vertical adjustments in the writing line.

Carrier: Moves from left to right carrying the printing mechanism across the paper.

Printing Mechanism: A small ball called an element or a daisy wheel printer containing the letters, numbers, and symbols. When a key is struck the element or daisy wheel prints the corresponding character. Since 1985 leading manufacturers have discontinued the use of an element in favor of the much faster daisy wheel which records 20 characters per second.

Carrier or Cursor Return Key: Returns the carrier or cursor to the beginning of a new line of type; continues to advance the lines as long as it is depressed.

Correction Key: On selected models backspaces to errors and raises lift-off tape to erase errors. On computers or word processors a delete key is used.

Index Key: Advances the paper to the next line without returning to the left margin.

On-Off Key: Turns the power on and off.

Backspace Key: Moves carrier to the left one space at a time; repeats as long as it is depressed.

Card Holder: Holds cards and envelopes against cylinder.

Shift Lock: Locks the shift key in position so that upper case letters are printed.

Space Bar: Advances the carrier to the right one space at a time; repeats as long as depressed.

Tab Set Key: Sets tab stops at designated points (i.e., for paragraph indentation).

Tab Key: Moves carrier to a preassigned point where a tab stop is set.

Tab Clear: Removes tab stops.

On modern typewriter keyboards, especially those built since 1985, many of the functions listed above are replaced by special code keys. If this is the case for your machine consult your manual.

Print Sizes

Typewriters come in two print sizes: pica and elite. Pica is the larger type size and prints 10 characters to an inch of type. Elite is the smaller size and prints 12 characters to an inch of type. A sheet of standard 8½″ × 11″ paper contains 85 pica characters to a line of type and 102 elite characters to a line of type. While this is standard for typewriters, word processors and computers may print a greater range of character sizes. Consult your operator's manual. The instructions in this book are based on pica or elite print sizes. If your machine prints larger or smaller characters your lines may not match those in the book. If this occurs, end your line after keying the last character in the line, strike your return key, and proceed to the next line. Do not stop to print your practice sessions until the lesson is completed.

THE IMPORTANCE OF A NEAT DESK

When you return to your typewriter, computer, or word processor, your work area should be arranged so that you can immediately begin your exercises. At the end of each session arrange your work area so everything you'll need is at your fingertips. Keep a stack of paper and this book right next to the keyboard.

Store reserve supplies away from the immediate keyboard area. At the end of each practice session, restore your work area to a state of neatness. ALWAYS LEAVE YOUR WORK AREA READY FOR A NEW START.

THE BASICS

1. Practice only after a period of rejuvenating rest. Typewriting is a skill and like many other skills it is learned by practice. The quality of your practice is directly related to your alertness. You will accomplish your best practice (or work) when you are not tired physically, mentally, or emotionally. By the same token, when you are on the job, approach your most difficult task when you are freshest. DO NOT PRACTICE WHEN YOU ARE TIRED OR SLUGGISH.

2. Plan a schedule that you can follow with maximum ease. It is important to stick to your schedule. You may find that you need to change the time of your practice session to preserve it. Make up missed practice sessions during previously scheduled alternate times. PRACTICE EVERY DAY! It is better to practice 15 to 20 minutes each day rather than skipping days or trying to cram all your practice sessions into one or two days. USE SPARE TIME FOR EXTRA PRACTICE.

3. Keep your work area neat and free of clutter with all your supplies handy. If you are using a typewriter you will need an ample supply of paper. Your keyboard should be approximately 26 inches from the floor. Arrange the keyboard so that the j-key is at the center of your body. Place the keyboard about 9 to 10 inches from your stomach. If you are using a word processor or

computer consult your manual for instructions on setting up files. Before you begin set up several files so that you will not use valuable practice time to do this.

4. You will need a timer to measure your speed. Use a timer with an alarm.

Margins

Think of your work on the printed page as a picture framed by balanced margins on all four sides. The white border is the frame and your printed text is the picture. Typists call these borders margins. When determining margins you will need to consider the amount of material you must record. Short letters and reports will take wider margins than lengthy documents. Keep the left and right margins equal. Place half of the line of type to the left of the center and the other to the right of center. For example, if you are about to key a very short letter of a few lines, since you do not wish to have your page appear skimpy of print, use wide margins so that the text appears in several lines. Use a 40-space line for this short piece. Divide the number of spaces by two ($40 \div 2$) and subtract the quotient (20) from the center of your line (42 for pica machines and 51 for elite). This is the number of spaces in your left margin. Add the quotient to the center to set your right margin. See your operator's manual for setting margin stops on word processors and computers.

COMMON MARGIN SETTINGS

Line Length	Center at 50 (Elite)		Center at 42 (Pica)	
	Left	Right	Left	Right
40 spaces	30	75	22	67
50 spaces	25	80	17	72
60 spaces	20	85	12	77
70 spaces	15	90	7	82

For ease in determining margins you may need to convert inches to spaces. Use the chart below:

CONVERTING INCHES TO SPACES

	4″	5″	6″
Number of inches in the line			
Pica spaces (10 per inch)	40	50	60
Elite spaces (12 per inch) rounded off	50	60	70

How to Insert Paper

If margin settings are to be accurate and provide the appropriate border around your work you will need to insert your paper correctly. To insert your paper properly, do the following:

1. Align the paper guide to correspond with zero on the paper guide scale. Since removing and inserting paper may push the paper guide out of place always check to be sure that it is properly aligned before inserting a new sheet of paper.

2. Place your paper at the left edge of the typewriter and pull the paper bail forward.
3. Pick up the paper with your left hand and place it lightly against the paper table with the left edge against the paper guide. Make sure it is straight.
4. Use your right hand to grasp the right cylinder knob and turn the paper quickly into position. When typing you will begin your text on line six or one inch from the top edge of the paper.
5. Place the paper bail against the paper to hold it in place.
6. If your paper is not even, use the paper release to make the needed adjustments.

If you are using one of the recently manufactured typewriters, do not pull the paper bail forward until after you have placed the paper on the paper table. When you pull the paper bail forward on these machines this action automatically activates the cylinder which turns to roll the paper into correct typing position. When you have finished typing a page, you can pull the paper bail forward to roll the paper automatically out of the machine.

To remove the paper from less automated typewriters, pull the paper release forward and lift the paper. Replace the paper release. If you are working on a computer or word processor consult your manual for instructions on loading the printer.

How to Set Line Spacing

The line space regulator controls the vertical spacing between lines. Typewritten lines can be single-, double-, or triple-spaced. When the line space regulator is set at 1 the cylinder advances one line each time the carriage is returned and leaves no blank spaces between the lines of type. This is single-spacing. When the line space regulator is set at 2 the cylinder advances twice and leaves one blank line between the lines of type. This is double-spacing. When the line space regulator is set at 3 for triple-spacing there are two blank lines between the lines of type. During many of your early practice sessions you will set your line space regulator at 1. Later, when you are typing paragraphs and timed writings, you will set your line space regulator for 2 or double-spacing.

Learning New Keys

When you complete this book you will have been introduced to the complete letter, number, and special character standard typewriter keyboard. This keyboard is the basis for computer and word processor keyboards. You will use the SEE IT, SAY IT, STRIKE IT method to learn each new key.

SEE IT, SAY IT, STRIKE IT

SEE IT

Place your hands on your lap, palms up, relaxed, fingers curving naturally, and locate the new key or keys with your eyes. Notice the surrounding keys, and record this visual image in your permanent memory for instant recall. "See It" refers to your eyes on the copy; see the letter in the text and recall the visual memory you made when looking at the keyboard.

SAY IT

Place your hands on the keyboard in the home row position (in early lessons it is permissible to look to see if your hands are correctly placed on the home row) as you place your eyes on the exercises in this book. Silently repeat the letter, number, or special character you are about to type.

STRIKE IT

Strike or flick the key as you say it.

To strike: Do not push the key or linger on it. Hit the key sharply, in the center, pulling inward toward your palm, and release it immediately. Strike the keys with even timing and equal force. The movement should be in the fingers. Move your arms and hands as little as possible.

To flick: Using a very slight inward motion flick the center of the key with the ball of your fingertip pulling inward; release.

If you are using an ultra-modern keyboard manufactured since the mid 1980s, you will flick your keys. If you are using a keyboard of the sort found on the IBM selectric series of the 60s, 70s and early 80s, you will strike your keys. For our purposes we will use the word "strike." If you follow the steps outlined here, you can learn the basic typewriter keyboard on any electric keyboard: typewriter, computer, or word processor.

BASIC INSTRUCTIONS

Review these instructions before beginning each practice session. The early lessons will remind you to do so but later it becomes your responsibility to follow these fundamental steps each time you approach a keyboard.

Now You Are Ready to Begin

Before the beginning of each session and throughout, each time you feel your alertness slipping, relax your mind and body. Use this relaxation exercise.

Prepractice Relaxation Exercise

Practice from a positive point of view. Clear your mind of depressing, negative thoughts. Think positive. Affirm success. Count your blessings and be thankful for them. You will be surprised at how acknowledging these little things we take for granted as blessings lifts your spirit, strokes your resolve, and improves your peace of mind.

Consciously begin your practice session with a positive point of view and an affirming attitude toward your self-image and ability to succeed. Now that your mind is relaxed and open to further challenge, RELAX YOUR BODY before you sit down to the keyboard:

1. Stand near your chair with your feet planted firmly, but comfortably, so that you stand and feel like a sturdy oak tree. Stand straight, tall, but do not tense up.
2. RELAX, allowing all of the tension to drain out of your body. Let your arms dangle loosely at your sides.
3. Imagine all of the tension draining downward from the top of your head, through your neck, shoulders, arms, torso, out through your hands and feet. You should feel relaxed, comfortable, but in charge.
4. Draw in a deep breath through your nose. Exhale slowly through your mouth for a period twice as long as the inhale. As you slowly exhale the tension, relax and reaffirm your positive attitude.
5. Repeat the breathing exercise two or three times until you feel sufficiently relaxed. When you feel the relaxation and positive attitude throughout your entire mind/body system, take your seat.

Posture

It is an axiom among typists that GOOD POSTURE decreases fatigue. Sit about eight inches from your keyboard. Place your feet firmly on the floor (remember the oak tree) and allow your body to lean slightly forward.

How to Place Your Hands and Fingers

Good technique in hand and finger placement is the hallmark of the best typist. With your upper arms extending from relaxed, straight shoulders, reach slightly upward to place your fingertips lightly on the home keys.

Left Hand	*Right Hand*
first finger f	first finger j
second finger d	second finger k
third finger s	third finger l
fourth finger a	fourth finger ;

Thumbs are tucked in and rest lightly on the space bar.
Relax. Your arms should be relaxed and still, the action of flicking or striking the keys is reserved for your fingers. As your fingertips rest lightly and comfortably on the home keys avoid resting your palms or wrists on the typewriter frame, keyboard, or table. Sloppy positions will lead to sloppy typing. Keep your upper arms and elbows near your body. Your forearms and hands are parallel to the slant of the keyboard while your elbows point a diagonal line to the floor. DO NOT ARCH YOUR WRISTS, BUT DO NOT LET THEM TOUCH THE KEYBOARD OR THE DESK.

From the point of contact with the key the motion of your finger is a downward one. Your finger extends downward from the curved second joint, STRIKING THE KEY SHARPLY, IN THE CENTER, AND RELEASING IT QUICKLY. Do not draw back, pulling the finger upward to strike or flick the key. Use a quick downward motion, securely depressing the key and quickly releasing the contact allowing the key and your finger to return to home key position. AFTER YOU HAVE RELEASED THE KEY, RETURN IMMEDIATELY TO HOME POSITION. Imagine that your release is so quick your finger gets back first and is waiting for the key to come up to meet it.

Practice Session One

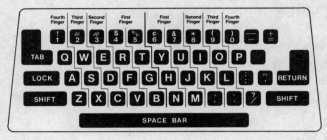

If you are using a typewriter, place your paper to the left front edge of your table or desk. For ease of reading, place your book in an upright tilted position to the right of your machine. If you are using electronic equipment, you will not need paper but you will need to place your book on the shelf with the keyboard and insert the appropriate diskette.

Now go back to the relaxation exercise on pages 16–17. Review and repeat it before starting this and each of your lessons.

Now that you are relaxed, take your seat and turn on the power. Place your hands on your lap, palms upward and watch your relaxed fingers curl into position. Remain relaxed as you lift your hands and turn them palms down. Hold your hands in a very relaxed manner, directly in front of you. Your hands should be even with the keyboard and poised to assume home key position. Now watch as you place your fingertips on the home keys: a s d f left hand and ; l k j right hand. This is the position your fingers always maintain when you are not keystroking.

THE SPACE BAR

Let your thumbs rest lightly on the space bar. You may strike it with either thumb; however, decide on one and use it. Keep your fingers on home key position without moving them and tap the space bar sharply, at the center, bouncing your thumb off instantly.

Watch your fingers carry out this pattern: See the space bar, say "space," strike the space bar once, then twice, then once, then twice. Repeat three times.

RETURNING THE CARRIER

Skill in returning the carrier or cursor to the beginning of the line is crucial to good typing. Master it at once. KEEP YOUR EYES ON THE PRINTED COPY as you extend the fourth finger of your right hand (the pinkie) to the return key. Try to develop a reach long enough and strong enough to allow you to keep the maximum number of fingers on the home keys. At a minimum always keep the j-finger in home position as you strike the return key. Return immediately to home key position.

Watch your finger as you see the return key, say "return," tap the key, and return immediately to home key position. Watch your finger carry out this pattern five or six times. Establish a permanent mental record of what you see. Return your eyes to the book and repeat the pattern several times without looking at your finger. YOU MUST NOW REFRAIN FROM LOOKING AT THE KEY. KEEP YOUR EYES ON THE BOOK, CALLING ON YOUR MENTAL VISION. You will soon master this important stroke. REMEMBER, SEE IT, SAY IT, STRIKE IT!

At first, "See It" always includes locating the key on the keyboard and initiating the first practice strokes. After you are instructed to return your eyes to the book "See It" then refers to the character in the book. Now you must SEE THE KEY WITH YOUR FINGERS.

MAINTAINING GOOD POSTURE IS KEY

Place your hands in your lap palms upward, relax.
Examine your posture and keep in mind that typing speed and accuracy *are both* affected by your posture. At the beginning of each session remember to sit with your body centered opposite the j-key, leaning slightly forward. Place your feet slightly apart, firmly planted. With straight wrists and curved fingertips on the HOME KEYS: left hand a s d f and right hand ; l k j. Now place your hands on your lap.

YOUR FIRST KEYSTROKES

Again, look at your keyboard, examine it carefully and locate the home keys. Make a visual record of what you see. You will see that the g, h, colon, and one or two other special character keys—this varies with the make and model of your equipment—are also on this row. However, your fingertips will rest on a s d f and ; l k j.

Locate the home keys with your eyes, noting them mentally. Watch as you place your hands in home key position. SEE IT, SAY IT, WATCH YOUR FINGER STRIKE IT:

```
a space s space d space f space space ; space l space k space j
return
```

Your line should look like this:

```
a s d f ; l k j
```

KEYSTROKE WITH AN EVEN RHYTHM. DO NOT BOUNCE BACK, STROKE FORWARD AND RELEASE. EYES ON YOUR COPY. SEE IT, SAY IT, STRIKE IT:
a space s space d space f space space ; space l space k space j space (return, repeat).

Good! Try that once more.

You have probably made some mistakes. Do not worry about them. Mistakes are natural at this stage. As you become more practiced your errors will decrease. DO NOT STOP TO CORRECT ERRORS DURING THE LESSONS. We will learn more about "typos" later.

Practice.

Keep your eyes on the copy as you practice the lines below. When you come to the end of the line of type DO NOT SPACE BEFORE

RETURNING. Key each line twice. Set your line spacing on single-space. Return twice between the pairs to establish a double-space before beginning the next line. Your lines will look like this:

```
fff fff fff ff ff ff fff ff (return, repeat)
fff fff fff ff ff ff fff ff (return twice)

jjj jjj jjj jj jj jj jjj jj (return, repeat)
jjj jjj jjj jj jj jj jjj jj (return twice)

fff jjj fjf fj fj fj fff fj (return, repeat)
fff jjj fjf fj fj fj fff fj (return twice)
```

HOME KEY PRACTICE

TYPE EVENLY, KEEP YOUR EYES ON THE TEXT. SEE IT, SAY IT, STRIKE IT. TYPE EACH LINE TWICE. STRIKE OR FLICK THE RETURN KEY TWICE AT THE END OF THE SECOND LINE TO ESTABLISH A DOUBLE-SPACE.

Follow this pattern as you keystroke the practice lines below.

```
fff jjj fff jfj fff jjj fjf jjj fff jjf
ddd kkk ddd kdk ddd kkk dkd kkk ddd kkd
sss lll sss lsl sss lll sls lll sss lls
aaa ;;; aaa ;a; aaa ;;; a;a ;;; aaa ;;a
asdf ;lkj asdf ;lkj asdf ;lkj asdf ;lkj

fads fdsa adfs dafs sfda sfad dsjf sdjf
fjad adfj djaf jfda afjd dfsa sfaj jsaf
kjfs sfjk ksdf dfsk djfa fajd djaf slka
kasl slka dfjl ldjf ldfj fldj lkjd jkdl
fsjl dfaf fjad ds;k ;dks k;as ;sak ak;j

ask a lad a sad dad ask a lad a sad dad
a dad; a lad; a fad; a salad; a sad lad
alas; a flask a dad falls; as a dad add
as ask al all sa sad la lad da dad asks

dad ask lad; as a salad; as a dad falls
```

THE HOME ROW

Relax and remove your hands from the keyboard, place them in your lap, palms upward, relaxed and naturally curled. Remember SEE IT, SAY IT, STRIKE IT means first to look at (see) the character you are about to practice, say the character silently, and then strike the character. For example, you will first see "f," then say "f" as you see and strike "f." What you say should sound like this: "fgf space fgf space." Always follow this pattern when employing the SEE IT, SAY IT, STRIKE IT method.

With your eyes find the location of the "g" key. Follow this pattern as you SEE IT, SAY IT, STRIKE IT with your eyes, forming a visual memory of the key locations:

```
fgf space fgf space fgf return
```

SEE IT, SAY IT, STRIKE IT with your finger: Now place your fingers in home key position. Do not move any other finger from home key position. All of the action is in your f-key finger. Remember to SEE IT, SAY IT, STRIKE IT as you employ your finger. Follow this pattern as you watch your f-finger reach to lightly tap without actually depressing the g-key and quickly return to home key position. You should be practicing the movement at this point without depressing the keys.

```
fgf fgf fgf
```

See the characters, say the characters, and strike the characters as you follow the pattern below and watch your f-finger strike and depress:

```
fgf fgf fgf
```

As you practice the lines below remember to SEE IT, SAY IT, STRIKE IT. Type each line twice. After the second keying of the line return twice to establish a double-space between the pairs. This is standard for all further practice sessions.

```
fgf fgf fgf fgf fgf fgf fgf fgf fgf fgf
fff ggg fgf gfg fff ggg gfg fgf fff ggg
fga fgs fgd fgf fgj fgj jjg jjg gfj fgf
gal fag gad gas gkg fgl fg; ;gf ;gf gfg
```

Practice the above until you have mastered it.
Relax and remove your hands from the home keys, placing them on your lap in the upright position. Use your eyes to locate the h-key on the home row and notice that it is controlled by the j-finger. Follow this pattern with your eyes.

```
jhj jhj jhj
```

Now place your hands in home key position. SEE IT, SAY IT, STRIKE IT with your finger: Watch your j-finger reach and lightly tap without actually depressing the h-key and without moving your hand or other fingers:

```
jhj jhj jhj
```

Now SEE IT, SAY IT, STRIKE IT as you depress the keys following this pattern: jhj jhj jhj
Keep your eyes on the book as you type the lines below. Do not look at your keys, but see the character in the book and say it. This should help you recall the visual memory you have just established and then strike it. You will say "jhj space jhj space" as you keep your eyes on the book and let your fingers do the typing:

```
jhj jhj hjh hjh jjj hhh hjh hjh jhj jhj
jjj jhj hhh jhj jjj jhj hhh jhj jjj jhj
jhj had hjh has jhj ash hjh had jhj ash
jh hash hj hall jh lash hj shad jh sash
```

```
fgfg gfgf jhjh hjhj jhjh hjhj jfgh ghfj
kafg d;jh kafg d;jh djah kf;h kafg d;jh

asdfg ;lkjh asdfg ;lkjh asdfg ;lkjh asdfg
gfdsa hjkl; gfdsa hjkl; asdfg ;lkjh jhfgh
```

Good work! If you have come to the end of this session before your allotted time is up, return to the beginning and keystroke it a second time through. If you have been unable to complete this session in the allotted time, go through it again at the beginning of your next session. If at the end of the second session you still have not completed the lesson, you may consider allotting more practice time. When you approach a lesson for a third time, then you may begin at the point where you left off in the previous session.

Master the drill lines above before proceeding to the next session.

Practice Session Two

Have you completed the relaxation exercise? Review and practice the foundation at the beginning of each practice session until it is automatic. The basic instructions outlined on pages 16–18 are the foundation from which you want to begin all of your typing.

Now that you have practiced the foundation you are ready to leave the home key position and reach to upper and lower key banks. As you progress you will find fewer instructions and more lines of practice. The basic instructions MUST be practiced until they become automatic. The instructions will be repeated in decreasing proportions in favor of motivational material and gems for the SUCCESSFUL CAREER PERSONALITY. So, do not just keystroke the lines, READ THEM. ESTABLISH NOW a habit of reading through completely everything you keystroke. The experts agree: IT HELPS TO PREVENT ERRORS WHEN YOU UNDERSTAND WHAT YOU ARE KEYBOARDING. Although in this early phase you will keystroke on the character level you should not be unaware of the units of thought.

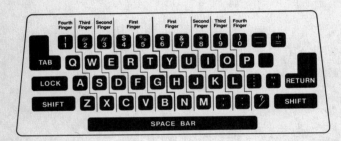

NEW KEYS: e u r i y t
Seated, relaxed, hands on lap, palms upward, locate the e-key. You will use your d-finger to control the e-key. See "e," say "e," and strike "e" with your eyes forming the process visually. Use this pattern:

ded ded ded

Remember, when you watch your finger locate and strike the key the first two or three times, touch the key lightly without depressing it. Now place your fingers in home key position and watch your d-finger as you see "ded space," say "ded space," and lightly tap "ded space" without depressing the keys.

ded ded ded

SEE IT, SAY IT, STRIKE IT with your fingers: Depressing the key this time, watch your finger as you keystroke

ded ded ded

Release the key quickly and return immediately to home row position as you keystroke. Quickly and accurately bounce your thumb off the space bar.

CHECKUP: Let's repeat the segment above but this time watch your f-finger. Is it remaining on the home key or does it move off the home key trying to assist the d-finger? Keep a relaxed f-finger in home key position as you reach up to strike the e-key. Remember, the goal: Keep ALL (a s d f ; l k and j too!) fingers in home key position as you strike the e-key. EYES ON COPY: SEE IT, SAY IT, STRIKE IT. Remember to type each line twice, double-spaced, and maintain good posture. THE BEST TYPISTS KEEP THEIR EYES ON THE COPY!

```
de de ed ed de de ed ed ded ded ded ee
de de ded ded dede dede dd ee eee dede
dead led lead dae; see fee lee fed sea
```

Remove your hands from the keyboard. By now you should automatically be resting your hands with palms upward on your lap. The u-key is controlled by your j-finger. Locate the u-key and SEE IT, SAY IT, STRIKE IT with your eyes following this pattern:

```
juj juj juj
```

Now, put your hands in home key position.
CHECKUP: Are your wrists low, but not touching the keyboard? Feet firmly planted? Elbows near body and relaxed? GOOD POSTURE IS A HALLMARK OF THE GOOD TYPIST!
Now that your eyes have formed a visual memory of the key's location on your keyboard, hands in position, watch your finger as you see "juj space," say "juj space," and strike "juj" without actually depressing the keys following this pattern:

```
juj juj juj
```

Now depress the key as you SEE IT, SAY IT, AND STRIKE IT
juj juj juj
CHECKUP: Is your k-finger remaining in home key position? What about your other fingers? They ALL should remain in home key position (including the thumbs) as you investigate the new key reaches. THE BEST TYPIST MAINTAINS QUIET HANDS AND FINGERS. KEEP THE ACTION IN YOUR FINGERS and keep your fingertips in home key position.
EYES ON COPY as you practice the lines below. Type each line twice, striking the return key twice after the second time to establish the double-space between the lines.

```
ju ju uj uj ju ju uj uj juj juj juj jjj
ju ju juj juj juju juju jj uu uuu juju
dud juj dud juj sue juj sue juj use ju
```

Relax. The r-key is controlled by the f-finger. Locate the r-key with your eyes and SEE IT, SAY IT, STRIKE IT.

```
frf frf frf
```

Place your hands in home key position. Watch your finger as you see "frf space," say "frf space," and lightly tap "frf space" without depressing the keys. Follow this pattern:

```
frf frf frf
```

SEE IT, SAY IT, STRIKE IT as you watch your finger keystroke:

```
frf frf frf
```

CHECKUP: What are your fingers doing when you strike "r"? Watch your finger as you repeat the line above without depressing the keys. This time practice keeping all other fingers QUIET!

EYES ON THE COPY as you practice the lines below and strive for good posture and quiet fingers. Take your time and do not worry about your errors. They will decrease as you increase your skill. Follow the practice guidelines presented here and watch your skill increase!

```
fr fr rf rf fr fr rf rf frf frf frf fff
fr frf frf frf frfr frfr ff rr rrr frf
frf juj drf juj rag kuj rad luj jar rf
```

Relax. The i-key is controlled by the k-finger. Locate the i-key with your eyes and SEE IT, SAY IT, STRIKE IT following this pattern:

```
kik kik kik
```

HANDS IN HOME ROW POSITION. Watch your k-finger reach up to lightly tap the i-key without depressing it:

```
kik kik kik
```

Depressing the keys, watch your finger keystroke:

```
kik kik kik
```

CHECKUP: What do you need to work on as you repeat the exercise above?

EYES ON THE COPY

```
ki ki ik ik ki ki ik kik kik kik ikki ik
kiki kiki ikik ikik kiki kik kiki iki k
lid rid did sid silk side fill sill ilk
```

Relax. The y-key is controlled with your j-finger. This reach is a little longer than the others, but you will quickly grow accustomed to it. Although it may feel awkward at first it will occur with ease as you follow the practice guidelines. With your eyes see "jyj," say "jyj," strike "jyj":

```
jyj jyj jyj
```

Place your hands in home key position and SEE IT, SAY IT, STRIKE IT without depressing as you watch what your other fingers do.

```
jyj jyj jyj
```

Practice this slightly longer reach several times. Reach, but do not leave home key position. Keep the reach in your j-finger. Now, depressing the key watch your finger as you see the key, say the key, strike the key:

```
jyj jyj jyj jyj
```

CHECKUP: Do you need to repeat the drill several times to work on technique? If not, go on.

EYES ON THE COPY

```
jyj jyj day say jay jury dry ray say ye
yj jy jyjy yjyj fray hay day lay kay ys
kyky jyjy jay jay say say yale days yes
```

Relax. Hands in lap, locate the t-key which is controlled by your f-finger and SEE IT, SAY IT, STRIKE IT with your eyes:

```
ftf ftf ftf
```

Hands in home row position as you watch your finger lightly tap

```
ftf ftf ftf
```

Depressing the key

```
ftf ftf ftf
```

CHECKUP: How is your posture? Are you alert to what your fingers are doing? Make sure your technique is correct.
Watch your f-finger lightly tap the t-key

```
ftf ftf ftf ftf
```

As you key the lines below remember: THE BEST TYPIST MASTERS TECHNIQUE FIRST THEN STRIVES FOR SPEED AND ACCURACY.

```
tft tftf fat dat jat kat fat rats taffs
taft raft left let use sit here ted tif
sat kat hat gate safe kate late fate te
```

TECHNIQUE DEVELOPMENT

Use the lines below to develop good technique. Strive for smooth, steady keystroking. Keystroke each line twice, double-spacing between by returning twice at the end of the second line.

```
shad ask alas dad flask sale salad lass
see fed fee lee use jell ash heeds held
dull soar dual oars safe juke suds dusk

rit sit lit ails ride set seat jets jars
rail lid file risk ate sat heed dread at
real dear fear jeer refill residue fell

ark dread refuse heat hilt kilt kite us
fake like lake slit fill risks sail fly
this that halt dish faith three threads

these taller safer irks to the rim dims
fret teeth tell as fast as usual seated
eat three tree that just ray lay day ask
```

```
lake dark risk fell three heard life is
this is a dry way to see the day are it a

jet letter hard their third head heard;
safety first says yard huge glue judge;
glad year yard jugs girls agree left it
```

Master the drill lines above before proceeding to the next lesson.

Practice Session Three

Are you relaxed? Is your foundation exercise becoming increasingly more automatic? Have you reviewed the notions of good technique presented so far, so that they are fresh in your mind?

NEW KEYS: Left and right shift keys, period, w, p, comma, q, and o.

Capital letters occur frequently throughout most typewritten material. To print a capital letter you will need to learn how to control the right and left shift keys. To capitalize a letter keystroked by a left-hand finger, hold down the right shift key with your semicolon finger and strike the letter. You must hold the shift down until you have depressed the letter you wish to capitalize.

With your eyes locate first the right shift key, look up and see ";" say ";" strike ";" reach down see shift say shift strike shift. Repeat.
YOUR GOAL: keep all fingers in home key position. Even if you are absolutely unable to complete the reach without slightly lifting the l- and k-fingers, NEVER remove the j-finger from home position when keystroking the right shift key. The more fingers you lift away from home row to depress this shift key, the greater the chance for errors. Hands in position. Watch your finger as you make the reach without depressing the keys: ; f shift and hold it, strike F, release, strike ; Repeat twice. Watch your fingers as you depress the keys:

;f; ;F ;F f;F

CHECKUP: Are you close to your goal? Repeat the line above and see.

KEEP YOUR EYES ON THE COPY AS YOU KEYSTROKE THE LINES BELOW

FF FfF fFf Fred Free FrF Fee Fef FRF Ss
dDd Dad Day Date S Sue SsS sEE Red Date
Ruth Fade Sad Said Safe Set Fat Fee Ask

To capitalize a letter typed by a righthand finger, you hold down the left shift key with the a finger and strike the letter. With your eyes, locate the left shift key and the a-key. See "a," say "a," strike "a." Reach down and see "shift," say "shift," depress "shift." Hold and return to home key. Repeat.
YOUR GOAL: KEEP ALL FINGERS IN HOME KEY POSITION
Watch your finger as you make the reach without depressing the keys:

a j, shift and hold it, keystroke A, release, strike a.
Watch your finger as you depress the keys:

```
aja aJ aJ jaJ
```

CHECKUP: Do you need to work on your goal? Repeat above.

EYES ON THE COPY

```
jJj aJa Jay aka aKa Kay Luke Kurt Harry
Jed Kit Let List Kilt Kate Late Hurts K
Harris Hulk Ida Is Late Ill Just Jams Y
```

Relax. The period is controlled by your l-finger. Find it with your eyes and SEE IT, SAY IT, STRIKE IT:

```
1.1 1.1 1.1
```

Hands in home key position as you watch your fingers lightly tap

```
1.1 1.1 1.1.
```

Keep your home key fingers quiet as you reach down to strike

```
.1. .1. .1.
```

EYES ON THE COPY as you practice the lines below. Remember TECHNIQUE is central to keyboarding success.

```
1.1 1.1 .1. .1. 11. L.L 1.L L.1 Sr. Dr.
... 111 ... 111 ... 111 L.L .L. Fr. Fr.
leak. just. adjust. ready. Rather. D.
```

Before you go further there are some very important rules you must always remember about the period. You must practice these rules until they occur automatically in your typing.

1. YOU ALWAYS SPACE TWICE AFTER A PERIOD WHEN IT OCCURS AT THE END OF A SENTENCE UNLESS IT OCCURS AT THE END OF A LINE.
2. SPACE ONCE AFTER A PERIOD FOLLOWING AN AB-BREVIATION OR AN INITIAL. Eyes on the copy as you practice the lines below. Avoid looking at your screen or line of type when you are keystroking.

```
I like Dale. Dale Likes it. Go to her.
At the sled. It is sure. Sue E. R. As.
Dr. Dale J. R. But he did. Easter. It.
```

You have learned a lot in a short period of time. Relax and take a short break of two or three minutes.

The w-key is controlled by the s-finger. Locate it with your eyes and SEE IT, SAY IT, STRIKE IT:

```
sws sws sws
```

Hands in home row position as you watch your finger tap lightly

```
sws sws sws
```

Now watch your finger depress the key and quickly return to home position

`sws sws sws`

CHECKUP: How is your technique? Fingers? Hands? Posture? Concentration? Repeat above and improve your technique.

EYES ON THE COPY

```
sws sws www sss www sws saw saw was was
Was why Why wish with Wade dew wait way
war wart will wish walk swap whip Wins.
```

Locate the p-key. You see that it is controlled by the semicolon finger. Practice the SEE IT, SAY IT, STRIKE IT pattern with your eyes:

`;p; ;p; ;p;`

Hands in position practice the pattern with a light tap:

`;p; ;p; ;p;`

Now depress the key:

`;p; ;p; ;p;`

CHECKUP: Are your wrists low, relaxed? Does your wrist rest on the keyboard or desk? Are your elbows close to your body? How is your posture? Are your l-, k-, j-fingers remaining in position? Does your thumb bounce off the space bar quickly? Repeat the exercise above as you remain alert to your technique.
EYES ON THE COPY mastered early is assured speed and accuracy later!

```
;;; ;p; ppp ;;; ;p; ;p; up up put put p;
dip rip tip apt apt pay pay lap lap lip;
Page Flop Paid Reply Deep Reap Happy App
```

The comma, like the period, is an essential element of good English and you will use it often. Notice that it is controlled by the k-finger. Follow the SEE IT, SAY IT, STRIKE IT pattern as you practice:

```
EYES: k,k k,k k,k
TAP: k,k k,k k,k
DEPRESS: k,k k,k k,k
```

CHECKUP: How is your technique?
EYES ON YOUR COPY as you practice the lines below. Remember to type each line twice and return twice before beginning the next line.

```
kkk k,k kkk k,k ,,, kkk k,k I will, I,
if he wishes, how, kit, jar, jot, jot,
K,K,K, k,k, Yes, Light, kik, kik, ,kik
```

Find the q-key and see that it is controlled by the a-finger. SEE IT, SAY IT, STRIKE IT:

EYES: aqa aqa aqa
TAP: aqa aqa aqa
DEPRESS: aqa aqa aqa

CHECKUP: Are you satisfied with your technique? Repeat above and improve your technique.

EYES ON THE COPY

aaa aqa qqq aaa aqa aqa que que quip qua
quid quit quayle quay quiet quart quarts
Guilt Equal Quest Quote Quell Quince Qui

Take a couple of minutes to stretch and relax. Let your arms and hands dangle at your sides as you shake the tension out of your hands onto the floor. Take several deep breaths.

See that the o-key is controlled by the l-finger. Practice the SEE IT, SAY IT, STRIKE IT pattern:

EYES: lol lol lol
TAP: lol lol lol
DEPRESS: lol lol lol

CHECKUP: Is your technique satisfactory? Repeat above and improve your technique.

PRACTICE GOOD TECHNIQUE BELOW

lol lll ooo lol old old odd odd low low
hold does foes oh oh lo sod sod for for
Does Foes Lose Lost Word Quote Loom Oil

TECHNIQUE DEVELOPMENT

Review the rules for the period, and practice them as you keystroke the lines below.

Joe Alma Pete Dee Lee Joyce Rose Hawaii
Fred Joseph Kate Donna Sue Lake Georgia
Friday Laura At Last For Your Trip Home

Her train is here. Stop and look left.
Dr. Fred S. Cook A. S. A. P. I see her.

This is her gift to Sue. Elsie J. Yee.

walk was jaws warm well were walk slows
Ask for what you will. See the saw. W
what was when wish where always dew dew

apt Pat paid tip pipe park page trap P.
peep Pope rope dope prep prepare praise
Pass the page here. Peep at the pages.

walk, there, take, pass, reply, always,
He is there, as you wish, let her, say,
Please Walter, do sit here. I., Karma,

qa Quality quite requires request equal
aqa quid quest quell equip quiet quite.

quota quart Quayle qualify queue Quinn

hood order odds oils odes oats oasis Oh
Follow the King to the door. Oleo food
room store todd should Ohio for told to

Master all of the drill lines in this session before proceeding to the next.

Practice Session Four

Are you completing the relaxation exercise automatically before you start the session?

Use the lines below to perfect good technique. Keyboard each line twice doubling-spacing between the pairs.

PATTERNS

```
SA;E ;EAS kiki kiki djif jdif frfr rfrf
lrli ilrs juju ujuj fuil fiul fior rofi
hpaw hpaw hwap pfrq pfrq frpj fgfg ielg
```

WORDS

```
tree Art silk Sol rid irk Use err Eat I
She Rae rail oak dark risk asked faith.
fresher fried fresh fish today title of

aches life cakes sets desk half data aa
atom head eases left fast; rake ride it
The hard rules; this hard day; heard it

faith jailer lode kiss iris items joked

tall hill that jut Sra Rita kale kilos I
Add it to the row. Go to the store. As

safety judge early huge skill great risk
steady adjust guard results full details
prepare, shelf goods, reply; depth; get,

walk dust shelf where always party flaps
prepare while Friday details Please just
law thaw wide pride agreed words profits
```

SENTENCES

```
Ella asked dad for the play field. Was
Read that letter. Their third; now you
The kid will rail, shriek as she falls.
```

```
Dad had told the jokes. They all were;
Dr. Drew left for Rome yesterday. Jeff
Pat saw the judge with Sue. Trust that
```

ERRORS

Begin now to pay attention to your mistakes. Learning to recognize your mistakes and working on correcting them will allow you to concentrate on the development of good proofreading skills and give you extra practice on difficult strokes. Some of your errors will occur randomly; others will follow patterns. Pay attention to any patterns you observe and work on perfecting your technique. Analyze your mistypes to break any pattern that contributes to consistency in errors.

Carefully proofread what you have just typed comparing your lines to those in this book. If you are working with a monitor, use a pencil and pad to note the error and line. If you are working on a typewriter remove your paper from the machine. As you proofread it on a flat surface draw a circle around each one of your mistakes.
Count it an error when:

1. Any stroke is incorrect. Omitted strokes are judged incorrect, strikeovers count as two errors. Do not space backwards (backspace) to correct errors. When you do so, you are compounding the error and must count it twice when figuring your speed.
2. Any punctuation is placed incorrectly or omitted.
3. Spacing after a word or after its punctuation is incorrect.
4. Any stroke is so light it does not show clearly.
5. One stroke is made over another.
6. A word is omitted.
7. A word is repeated.
8. Words or characters are transposed.
9. A direction or rule about spacing, indenting, and so on, is violated.

Only one error is charged to any one word, no matter how many errors it may contain except in the case of strikeover, then two errors are counted.

ERROR CORRECTION DRILL

Pay close attention to the instructions in this drill. Refer to it until you know it very well. You will use it often in the sessions to come. Take care in finding your miskeys since the typist is responsible for error-free work. GOOD PROOFREADING SKILLS ARE AN ESSENTIAL ELEMENT OF GOOD TYPING. As you key your error correction drill, concentrate on accuracy and technique development. After you have carefully noted your errors, practice the word where the mistype occurs as well as the words surrounding it. For example, if you make an error in "fate" typing it "faet" and "fast" came before it and "late" followed it, your pair of lines will look like this:

```
fast fate late fast fate late fast fate
fast fate late fast fate late fast fate
```

Keystroke two correct lines of this combination for every word in which you make an error. This is the error correction drill.

Do not become overly concerned about the number of errors you are making. Put your energy into practicing the reaches correctly. It is normal to make mistakes in this early stage. As your skill increases your errors will decrease. Do not focus on the errors; focus on the positive results you will get from this practice. Remember the error correction drill is the only practice that you will design specifically for you.

As you keystroke the lines of this drill, type evenly and calmly. Strike and release your keys in one motion with quick, sharp, centered strokes.

Conclude each of the succeeding sessions with this error correction drill.

Practice Session Five

Did you complete the relaxation exercise? As you work on the patterns in this session, remember to release your keys quickly, moving your hands and arms as little as possible. Do not look up when you return the carrier or cursor. As you watch your fingers look out for humped wrists! Throughout this session concentrate on typing evenly and calmly as you strive for smooth, steady keystroking.

NEW KEYS: Tab, c, v, n, m, b, z

The tabulator key will play an important role in your keyboarding. Much of the material you type will appear in paragraph form. Remember these important rules for typing paragraphs:

1. Precede a single-spaced paragraph with one blank line. The first word may be either indented five spaces or blocked at the margin.
2. When a paragraph is double-spaced, indent the first word five spaces. Use the tabulator key for this indention. The tabulator key moves the printing point 5, 10, 15, or any number of spaces in one keystroke.

Many electronic keyboards now have special code keys and instructions for setting a tabulator key stop. Consult your manual for instructions on setting the tab stop on your equipment.

SETTING THE TABULATOR STOP

1. Confirm margin settings.
2. Clear out all previous tab stops according to the instructions in your manual or by holding down the tab clear key as you return the carrier from the right margin.
3. Set new tab stops by spacing forward the number of spaces you wish to indent. Five is most often used in paragraph indention.
4. Set your tab stop five spaces from your left margin. On some machines this is accomplished by depressing the tab set key.

Now that your tab stop is set you are ready to practice the keystroke. The tabulator key is controlled by your a finger.

SEE IT, SAY IT, STRIKE IT

```
EYES: a tab, return, a tab, return, a tab, return
TAP: a tab, return, a tab, return, a tab, return
DEPRESS: a tab, return, a tab, return, a tab, return
```

CHECKUP: Are your fingers remaining in home key position? On the sleek, modern keyboard the tab key is within easy reach. Older models require a longer stretch. If your keyboard requires a long reach to the tabulator key, try to keep the f-finger anchored on home row. Each time your finger leaves home position, the probability of misstrikes increases.

PARAGRAPH PRACTICE

Keep your fingers in home key position as you practice the lines below. Review the rules for paragraphs. Key each paragraph twice before going to the next. Use the tab key to indent each paragraph five spaces.

We feel that your request is just as we would ask. You are clearly alert to the large store.

      Prepare your orders today so that they are ready for the trip. People who work like you are highly regarded.

      The ship took a short trip last April. The sale will yield a good profit.

      Use the d-finger for the quick downward reach to strike the c-key.

SEE IT, SAY IT, STRIKE IT

EYES: dcd dcd dcd
TAP: dcd dcd dcd
DEPRESS: dcd dcd dcd

EYES ON THE COPY AS YOU WATCH YOUR TECHNIQUE GROW

Remember, each line twice, double-spacing between the pairs.

dcd dcd dcd ded dedc dedc dcde dedc ded
dedc cded ecde ecde edce edce dedc cded
acts colt itch cat each case space case

      Use your f-finger for the easy reach to the v-key.

CHECKUP: Are your elbows close to your body? Are you alert to good technique? How are your feet placed? Are your legs crossed? Or, are your feet firmly planted on the floor? Are you practicing concentration, bringing your mind immediately back when it wanders?

SEE IT, SAY IT, STRIKE IT

EYES: fvf fvf fvf
TAP: fvf fvf fvf
DEPRESS: fvf fvf fvf

EYES ON THE COPY

fvf fvf fvfv fvfv vfvf vfr rfv vfr rfvf
frv fvr frv frvf frvf rvfr rvfr very Vv
Dr. Vick is the vet for Velvet. Vi vats

      Use your j-finger to control the n-key. This is another quick reach down to the first bank of keys. Improve your technique as you master the strokes below.

SEE IT, SAY IT, STRIKE IT

```
EYES: jnj jnj jnj
TAP: jnj jnj jnj
DEPRESS: jnj jnj jnj
```

EYES ON THE COPY

```
jnj jnjn jnjn jnj nju ujn ujnj njuj ujn
jnuj jnuj jnju jnju ujuj jnjn juju jnjn
and Dan rain rink nine pen net Len sins
```

The j-finger also controls the m-key.

SEE IT, SAY IT, STRIKE IT

```
EYES: jmj jmj jmj
TAP: jmj jmj jmj
DEPRESS: jmj jmj jmj
```

As you type the lines below make reaches between the third and the first row without having your fingers pause on the home row.

EYES ON THE COPY

```
jmj jmj jmjm jmju jmju jujn jnjm jmnj jm
jam Jane jump joints jammed many flames
mom arms roam meet meat home clam mocks
```

Use the f-finger to control the b-key.

SEE IT, SAY IT, STRIKE IT

```
EYES: fbf fbf fbf
TAP: fbf fbf fbf
DEPRESS: fbf fbf fbf
```

EYES ON THE COPY

```
fbf fbf fbfb fbfb fbfr frfb frfb fbfr b
fbf fgb fbv fbr fbt fbf fgb fbr fgb fbt
bulb brush bake blue February September
```

Your a-finger controls the z-key.

SEE IT, SAY IT, STRIKE IT

```
EYES: aza aza aza
TAP: aza aza aza
DEPRESS: aza aza aza
```

EYES ON THE COPY

```
aza aza azaz azaz azdaq azaq aqaz aqaz az
aaa zzz aza zee zone Zola zeal size daze
doz. zinc raze jazz quiz seize seize zoo
```

TECHNIQUE DEVELOPMENT

Paragraph practice: Type each paragraph twice. Remember, a blank line precedes singled-spaced paragraphs.

I am glad to confirm at last that I will be able to see you in the very near future. Perhaps near the end of the month.
     When you are free stop at my desk for the new information. You will be delighted.

CHECKUP: Are your feet firmly planted? Imagine your feet flat against the floor a few inches apart comfortably placed, registering the assurance and security of an oak tree.

cakes call each Chad cook case quick cat
office aches calm cite charm Cade checks
jacket acid could reach practice quickly

vase verse have veto vest very Davis vie
via vat Vera Vast volume Van David loves
lava Viola victor vividly vow visit vote

new news then den net on ten tens tent n
wine wind neon none annoy noun Nic inane
rink went winning Nancy fun men women in

male must make most melds much maim mars
same dimes charm jam mare mess male miss
Most of the Maine coast is rugged. May;

baby job bag Bob boss ebbs barb Barb Bo
debt back bulb bull bend number brown b
bush Dr. Ben brown A brown box above be

zebra Zelda zap zoom grizzly fuzzy Zeke
zilch whiz zany lazy zest zigzag crazy.
There are a zillion zebras at the zoos.

     Review the instructions on pages 35–36; proofread carefully and complete the error correction drill for all sections of Technique Development.

Practice Session Six

Let your elbows hang loosely at your sides, while you keep your wrists low and feet firmly anchored. Type evenly and smoothly. Do not look up when you return the cursor. By curving your finger under when you are reaching downward like d to c or j to m, you can make these reaches without moving your hands at all. This will give you greater accuracy and speed.

NEW KEYS: / ? x - : margin release code keys

The diagonal is controlled with the semicolon (;) finger.

SEE IT, SAY IT, STRIKE IT

```
EYES: ;/; ;/; ;/;
TAP: ;/; ;/; ;/;
DEPRESS: ;/; ;/; ;/;
```

EYES ON THE COPY

```
;;; /// ;;; /// ;/; ;/; ;/; /;/ /;/ /;/
and/or us/them we/the yes/no now/later;
n/c P/Q is/or King/Sing Gate R/U quire/
```

CHECKUP: Did you complete the prepractice relaxation exercise before beginning this session? Watch your elbows. Keep them hanging loosely by your sides. They should not swing out.

The ? mark is the shift of the / and is also controlled by the semicolon finger and the a finger to shift. Leave two spaces after a question mark at the end of a sentence.

SEE IT, SAY IT, STRIKE IT

```
EYES: ; a shift? ; a shift? ; a shift?
TAP: ; a shift? ; a shift? ; a shift?
DEPRESS: ; a shift? ; a shift? ; a shift?
```

EYES ON THE COPY

Strive to keep your fingers in home key position, your hands, wrists and arms quiet. KEEP THE ACTION IN YOUR FINGERS.

```
;?; ;?; ;?; ?;? ?;? ;?;? ?;?; ;/;? ;/;?
/;p? /;p? /;p? p;/? p;/? p;/? ;p?/ ;p?/
Who? Are you ready? Can you be? She?
```

The x-key is controlled by your s-finger.

SEE IT, SAY IT, STRIKE IT

EYES: sxs sxs sxs
TAP: sxs sxs sxs
DEPRESS: sxs sxs sxs

EYES ON THE COPY

sxs sxs sxs xsx xsx xsx swsx swsx sxsws
sxsw sxsx sxsx xsxs xws xws wsx wsx axe
tax fix lax exit Rex sox box expect mix

The hyphen is used to connect the parts of compound words like up-to-date. Avoid using the hyphen to divide words at the end of a line. If the word will not fit on the line you are working on, move it to the next line. Word processing programs with wraparound automatically place long words at the beginning of the new line of print.

Important rules governing the hyphen:

1. DO NOT SPACE BEFORE OR AFTER TYPING HYPHENS: up-to-date
2. TWO HYPHENS TYPED IN SUCCESSION MAKE A DASH: Never--never!

Use your semicolon finger to control the hyphen (-).

SEE IT, SAY IT, STRIKE IT

EYES: ;-; ;-; ;-;
TAP: ;-; ;-; ;-;
DEPRESS: ;-; ;-; ;-;

CHECKUP: Keep your elbows close to your body as you reach to key the hyphen. Make the stretch with your semicolon finger. In the beginning you may need to slightly lift the l-finger. With practice, however, the goal is to keep your fingers in home key position as you stretch and make the reach. Repeat the lines above.

EYES ON THE COPY

;-; ;-; ;-; -;- -;- -;- ;-;- ;-;- -;-;-
;p-p; ;/;p- ;/;p- -p;?/ -p;?/ -p;?/ ;p-
twenty-one fifty-two He wept--it meant.

The colon is integral to the business letter. Most business letters use the colon to punctuate the salutation: Dear Bette: The colon is used to set off parts of sentences, to clarify, and to sequence. It often occurs in documents you must keyboard. Leave two spaces after a colon except when you are reporting time.

The colon is the shift of the semicolon finger.

SEE IT, SAY IT, STRIKE IT

```
EYES: ;a shift: ;a shift: ;a shift:
TAP: ;a: ;a: ;a:
DEPRESS: ;a: ;a: ;a:
```

EYES ON THE COPY

```
;:; ;:; ;:; ;:;/ ;:;/ ;:/; ;:?; ;:?; ;:
pot: For Example: The Following: ;:;
Dear Mr. Jon: Help me: I am prepared:
```

There may be times when you will need to use your margin release. On many keyboards the margin release key is controlled with the a-finger. On many others it is operated via a special code key. Many electronic keyboards contain special code keys for a range of operations. Consult your machine's manual for instructions on the operation of any code keys on your keyboard. There are no special fingering requirements for code keys placed outside of the basic typewriter keyboard. Obviously, left-hand code keys should be operated with left fingers and right-hand code keys with right-hand fingers. If the code is activated by one of the keys of the basic keyboard, use correct fingering to depress it.

TECHNIQUE DEVELOPMENT

The keys on the modern keyboard are very sensitive. You need only touch them slightly or lightly to make them print. Strike the keys in the center to avoid depressing surrounding keys. Use a quick, light, centered stroke as you key the lines below.

```
; / ; / ; / ; ;p;/; ;p;/; ;p;/; /;/ do/
Opal/ ;//; nuts/bolts c/d if we/ if we/
Kate/Olga his/her accept/except did he/
```

```
; ? ; ? ; ? ;p?/; ;p?/; ;p-?; ;p-?; ;?/
Will they go? Are you ready? Are you?
Turkey? Are you a young worker? Know?
```

```
sxs sxs sxsx wsxs wsxs wsxs wasp wants?
Fax x-ray laxative luxury Lux Xerox axe
Extra except example examine expose exp
```

```
wage-earner loosely-hung-thin dress at-
Knitting-factory places you--can they--
The green pack--the one there--is sold.
```

```
;:; ;:; curfew: West: airports; visa:
;:;: Dear John: Dear Madam: Dear Sir:
affords: void; belief: riots; basics:
```

Paragraph practice: Type each paragraph twice before going on to the next. Review instructions for paragraph practice. Use the tabulator key to indent five spaces.

        We feel that our request--the one we phoned in
yesterday--qualifies us for the first prize ticket. Please let
us know exactly where we stand.
        The store is always very crowded. We suggest that you use
the mail order facility--the one that stocks the very same
goods.
        Without further delay we are moving to the new, larger, more
spacious office suite.

Review and complete the error correction drill for all lines in Technique Development.

Practice Session Seven

By now you are probably wondering what your rate of typing is in words per minute (wpm). In this session you will learn how to figure your speed in 30-second speed bursts, and on one- and three-minute timed writings. You will need to use your timer now. Remember, do not use a clock that requires you to look away from your text. Your concentration must be on the typing. Looking away from your text to keep track of the time is very distracting. It will slow you down and promote errors, and your score will not accurately reflect your ability. Use a timer with an alarm. During the timed writing your goal is to keep your eyes on the copy while you concentrate on technique: SPEED AND ACCURACY.

CHECKUP: Did you complete the foundation exercise? It is very important to be relaxed when you are keyboarding a timed writing. If you are already tense, your nervousness may become great enough to hamper your performance. If you are relaxed at the start, your tension can be converted to useful energy allowing you to surmount challenges with skill and competence. ALWAYS TAKE A MOMENT TO RELAX BEFORE BEGINNING TO KEYBOARD. Make this habit part of your career personality.

MEASURING YOUR SPEED

1. Set your timer for the number of minutes or seconds you are going to keystroke.
2. Type for the exact number of minutes you have set the timer. Stop immediately at the sound of your timer.
3. Every 5 strokes counts as one word. The number of words in a line are marked off by the horizontal scales along the bottom of the text. In any text of more than one line the words are cumulatively totaled at the end of each line. Use your tabulator key for paragraph indention. Count five strokes or one word for each paragraph indention.
4. Divide the words typed by the minutes typed. If you typed 26 words in 2 minutes you are typing at a rate of 13 wpm. If you typed 45 words in 3 minutes you are typing at a rate of 15 wpm. However, if you typed 50 words in 2 minutes you are typing 25 wpm.
5. If you finish the text before the timer sounds, start over again without pause or hesitation. Continue keyboarding the timed writing repeatedly as many times as possible without looking up until the time has elapsed.
6. Return at the end of each line.

When figuring your typing speed, count every five strokes including spaces as one word. You will use the cumulative word count at the end of the line and the horizontal scale at the bottom to accomplish this. Suppose you typed the following for 1 minute.

```
We know that you are going to have great         (9)
sales with his new product. It is by far our    (18)
best idea. You will be pleased, I am sure.      (26)
    1       3       5       7       9
```

If you typed this for one minute you are typing at the rate of 26 wpm. If you completed only two lines when the buzzer sounds you typed 18 wpm. If you got to the word will, add 18 to 3 giving you a total of 21 wpm.

If you are typing for 2, 3, or 5 minutes, you divide the total number of words typed by the number of minutes typed. For example, if you typed for 2 minutes and completed the entire paragraph, started over and got to "product," you will add $26 + 9 + 4 = 39$ divided by $2 = 19$ wpm.

Using the method above your speed reflects the gross words per minute you are typing. Count your errors and you will have your speed and errors. Try to keep the number of errors you make under one per minute. For example, if you typed the above through twice in two minutes ($26+26=52\div2=26$), your speed score is 26 gross words per minute (gwpm). Perhaps you made 2 errors. Your score is 26 wpm with 2 errors. You are making an error per minute. As in all of the previous drills, when you are typing a timed drill it is very important to end your line of type at the same point the line of type ends in this book. If you fail to do this, you will find it difficult to figure your speed accurately. Do not type the cumulative number count at the end of each line.

ACCURACY SPEED ACCURACY (ASA) DRILLS

Pay close attention to the instructions here. You will use the ASA drill in every lesson to come. Review the instructions each time you do the drill until you know them exactly.

Set your timer to 30 seconds for this drill. In the 30-second drill, figure your speed by multiplying the total number of words typed by 2. For example, if you type 6 words during the 30-second drill, your speed score is 12 wpm.

Type a complete ASA drill on each sentence below in this way: Setting your timer for 30 seconds try to type the sentence through as many times as you can in the 30 seconds while striving for the best technique possible, thus the most accurate typing you can accomplish. Avoid poking along. Your goal is to type as fast as you can without making an error. Your priority is ACCURACY. At the sound of the timer STOP IMMEDIATELY! Proofread, count your errors, and figure your speed. Complete the error correction drill: Type two correct lines of each word you find in error. Now set the timer for 30 seconds, but this time concentrate on SPEED, allowing your fingers to fly across the keys without concern for accuracy. You want to see just how fast you can go. When the timer sounds count your errors and figure your speed. You will probably make more errors in the speed drill when you stretch your fingers out to see just how fast you can go. Push as fast as you can go, but DO NOT LOSE CONTROL. Now that you have seen just how fast your fingers can go, slow down a bit and concentrate on ACCU-RACY again. On the second accuracy drill, which is the third part of the ASA drill on the same sentence, increase your speed and keep your errors down. Concentrate on achieving the very best technique at the highest rate of speed. Your goal is to type the entire 30 seconds as fast as you can without making an error and this time with several more strokes than the first time. At the sound of the timer, figure your speed and accuracy.

Complete an ASA drill on each of the sentences below before going on to the next. Remember always complete an error correction drill following the first Accuracy timing. If you finish the sentence before the time is up, type it again and continue typing it until the timer sounds.

The purpose of the ASA drill is to gain a few strokes of speed with each drill and to decrease your errors with each drill.

```
The quota will be filled in enough time.                    (8)
It is your duty to type as well as possible, says he.      (10)
As you hit the keys, do not move your elbows.               (9)
        2       4       6       8      10      12
```

CHECKUP: Are you worrying about your mistypes? You will need to risk some mistakes at this stage. It is better to risk errors now than to break your rhythm by looking away from your text. THE FASTEST TYPISTS KEEP THEIR EYES ON THE COPY. DO NOT WATCH YOUR FINGERS!

TIMED WRITINGS

Speed goals: 10 to 15 wpm
Error limit: 7 to 9

ONE-MINUTE TIMED WRITINGS

Take three, one-minute timed writings on the paragraph below. After each timed writing complete an error correction drill. Concentrate on speed and accuracy. Try to type as fast as you can without making an error. Use one-minute timed writings to achieve control. Your goal: To type for one minute without an error.

```
We will be glad to arrange the loan you wish. The check of your   (12)
credit revealed a very good record. It is good to know that       (23)
there are people like you in the business. Thank you for          (34)
choosing our bank.                                                (38)
        2       4       6       8      10      12
```

TWO-MINUTE TIMED WRITINGS

Take two, two-minute timed writings on the paragraph below. Do an error correction drill following each timing. Try to increase your speed and decrease your errors.

```
It is a pleasure to send you a copy of our book on how to begin to   (12)
develop your career personality. Many years of practice and          (24)
research have gone into the development of this book, and we          (36)
know the book will be of great help to you. You will see that it      (48)
is well organized into topics and chapters. We are sure that         (60)
our readers will find the index very helpful. You will be happy      (72)
you decided to order now.                                            (77)
        1        3        5        7        9        11
```

CHECKUP: Hold your fingers motionless in home position as you tap the space bar in the center and bounce off. Use a quick, stabbing motion as you extend your ";" finger to lightly tap the center of the return key, zipping it back to home key position.

THREE-MINUTE TIMED WRITING

Take two, three-minute timed writings on the paragraph below. Proofread and score each timed writing and complete an error correction drill. Try to improve your score the second time.

```
As complex as word processors are, a good typist can learn how   (12)
to operate these machines. Word processing personnel claim       (24)
that it is often easy to train a good typist to operate these     (36)
modern business wonders. However, you must first be an expert    (48)
typist; then you must possess good English skills; and           (60)
finally, you must know how to proofread. Remember, it is the      (72)
the responsibility of the typist to submit correct work.         (83)
        1        3        5        7        9        11
```

CHECKUP: Are you making too many errors? Concentrate on each reach, and practice, practice, practice. Remember, concentration is the hallmark of the good typist. When your mind wanders, bring it back immediately.

The error and speed goals above are scores for you to strive for. Your score may be higher or lower. Do not worry; continue to practice and you will reach your goals. Each of us has a different capacity and a different potential for reaching that capacity. We also get there at different rates of speed. Use the goals as guidelines.

When typing long words like "responsibility" for the first time, type at the stroke level until you have mastered the word.

Master the material above before proceeding to the next session.

Use your spare time as an opportunity to get extra practice on the material above. MASTER TECHNIQUE and you MASTER SPEED AND ACCURACY. Remember, DO NOT THINK SPEED, THINK SMOOTH.

Practice Session Eight

SKILL DEVELOPMENT

Use this practice session to build your speed and accuracy. Concentrate on technique and push past your present speed and accuracy level. As you key each of the lines below, maintain a smooth and steady pace. Speed up the second time you type the line.

ALTERNATE HANDS

so or is so to on if do me am go by an to he us
but oak eye fit may fir dog tie fix it tie sues
emblem down auditors profit ivory make firm was
She could not make profit nor quota on the fur.

REACHES

sum race kill city just loop dismay by women it
hill uphill visual ornament music myth presents
lump country increase pony argued army alive of
flowers lusty human expect seven front David is
The student gave her a plaque for the new wall.

TECHNIQUE

answer swears ratio water arson army ark acid A
polled train repeat there swift swell salvo Sal
lucky juicy sting lull taping tenure Sidney can
league thereafter theater tires taken tamed too

imagine men mine mine numbers mind must melds N
adjust Switzerland Saturday merchants dates sat
cold older polite swallow follow oils Olay Olds
manage flowers station notions France Vivian Is

COMBINATIONS

as safe assassin seal stake arisen arson saves.
Ask salaries speak state sales saint sat saps S
save standards arrested smash arrest As has sit
Assure the staff, their salaries are very good.

Edith edit editor edges need educate Den demons
deep desk despair demolition demonstrate desire
kindness kites Kings kilos Kismet kinder keel K
lesson long common prone phone only once unions

SENTENCES

Under the circumstances, he will go too. I do.
A number of changes were necessary for success.
Has Malcolm been to the Ice Cream parlor today?
He assigned new--but less costly--books to Ava.

CHECKUP: Did you complete the error correction drill? Are you proof-reading carefully making sure that you find all of your miskeys. IT IS THE TYPIST'S JOB TO PRODUCE CORRECT TYPESCRIPT. Develop excellent proofreading habits now. Do not overlook errors.

ACCURACY SPEED ACCURACY

Review the instructions for the ASA drills on page 46. Do an ASA drill on each of the sentences below. Always complete the error correction drill following the first accuracy timing. Since an individual sentence comprises the entire ASA timed writing the totals at the end of each sentence are not cumulative.

There is a time for everything.   (6)
Pay all of your bills with our printed checks.   (9)
Use firm, brisk strokes as you enjoy control over the keys. (12)
Two spaces follow a period at the end of a sentence.   (10)
                2   4   6   8   10   12

TIMED WRITING

Speed range: 10 to 15 wpm
Error limit: 7 to 9

Complete the timed writings below, proofread, figure your speed, and complete the error correction drill following each timing.
Take three, one-minute timed writings on the paragraph below. Try to type as fast as you can on each try without making an error.
Take three, three-minute timed writings on the paragraph below.
DO NOT PROCEED TO THE NEXT TIMED WRITING UNTIL YOU HAVE COMPLETED THE ERROR CORRECTION DRILL.

Thank you very much for sending me your change of address and   (12)
telephone number. You see, ever since you worked on my   (22)
automobile it runs worse than it did before I came in to your   (33)
shop. Your work in the past has always been very good. Perhaps   (45)
you will want to review the work to determine what is wrong.   (56)
    When I brought the car in to you I explained that it was   (67)
stalling at signal lights and on other complete stops. Since   (79)
you worked on it the engine is now also cutting off at slow   (90)
speeds. Additionally, it is very hard to start in the morning,   (102)
just when I need it the most. Bill, in the past your work has   (113)
been of such high quality, I am wondering if perhaps you   (124)
allowed one of your young trainees to do the work. At any rate, (136)
for the first time during our long business association the   (147)

work from your shop is not satisfactory. Will you please call   (159)
me so that we can arrange a time to meet and discuss this   (170)
problem?   (172)

     2   4   6   8   10   12

Master the drill lines in this session before proceeding to the next.

Practice Session Nine

In the previous sessions you have learned and practiced the entire letter keyboard. In the next sessions you will learn the number and special character keys. On the modern keyboard these keys are an easy reach from home row position and will slow your pace little when you concentrate. Strike and release your keys in one motion with quick, snappy strokes. Type evenly and calmly as you strive for smooth, steady keystroking.

New Keys: 1 4 5 8 9

CHECKUP: Strike the return key quickly, and return to home position without looking up. YOU ARE A TOUCH TYPIST.

Use the a finger to control the 1-key. If your machine does not have a 1-key use the small L (l).

SEE IT, SAY IT, STRIKE IT

EYES: ala ala ala
TAP: ala ala ala
DEPRESS: ala ala ala

CHECKUP: Keep your wrist low, fingers curved. When you make the reach to the fourth key bank, keep all other fingers on the home keys. Concentration is essential. When your mind wanders, bring your attention back immediately.

EYES ON THE COPY

aql aql lqa lqa aqla aqla lqal lqal aql alla ll
qalq a.l l.a l.ll llll l add l boy l girl l day
one l two l three l ll women l pathway l.l..ll

   The f-finger controls the 4-key.

SEE IT, SAY IT, STRIKE IT

EYES: f4f f4f f4f
TAP: f4f f4f f4f
DEPRESS: f4f f4f f4f

EYES ON THE COPY

f4f f4f 4f4 4f4 fr4f fr4f 4rf4 4rf4 f44f r4f4f
fast 4 fast 14 plus 44 fell 41 444 4.4 4:44 4,
The 44 years and the 14 days but not 414.14141

   The 5-key is controlled by the f-finger.

SEE IT, SAY IT, STRIKE IT

EYES: f5f f5f f5f
TAP: f5f f5f f5f
DEPRESS: f5f f5f f5f

EYES ON THE COPY

f5f f5f f5f fr5f fr5f ft5f ft5f fr5t ft5r frt5
five 55 four 51 favor 54 Florence 15 floor 451
5 days 4 plays 1 chance 41 stools 45 brings 54

The 8-key is controlled by the k-finger.

SEE IT, SAY IT, STRIKE IT

EYES: k8k k8k k8k
TAP: k8k k8k k8k
DEPRESS: k8k k8k k8k

EYES ON THE COPY

k8k k8k 8k8 8k8 8k, 8ki 8ki, ,8ki ki8k ,8ik 88
8 kilos 18 kites 85 dates 48 spaces 184 shades
8 and 4; 1 and 8; 15 and 84 41 and 58 85.41 81

Use your l-finger to control the 9-key.

SEE IT, SAY IT, STRIKE IT

EYES: 191 191 191
TAP: 191 191 191
DEPRESS: 191 191 191

EYES ON THE COPY

191 191 919 919 lol9 lol9 lol9 lol9 9ol.9 ol9.
91 minutes 95 times 965 busses 45,159 56.9 994
July 19, 1991 and 1999 and 1995 or 1994 A 1996

TECHNIQUE DEVELOPMENT

As you practice the lines below—typing each line twice, double-spacing between the pairs—hold your hands directly over the home keys; avoid slanting your fingers.

1 peach 14 seats 41 deceits 1991 chores 91,191
1558 leisure 891 dewdrop 581 treason 1851 blew
14 15 18 19 91 94 95 98 99 1144 55 88 99 81 51

414-415 doorknob 549-451 character 815-558 Tee
14,589 misery 45 Henry Street 48 items 49 ways
41 facts 94 cases 54 vines 84 cans 415 Rye St.

589 145 458 985 859 415 189 919 145 158 189 11
981 891 845 458 914 911 955 589 458 145 914 81
4199 5498 1489 9548 5189 4918 5814 9158 1985 8

Please send 14 tickets in 14 envelopes for the 15 plays.
Their 5555 seats were filled with the 5555 arrangements.
The new airplanes flew the route in 5 hours, 19 minutes.

Proofread carefully, and complete the error correction drill.

ACCURACY SPEED ACCURACY

Complete the error correction drill following the first accuracy drill. Strive for fewer errors and higher speeds on the second accuracy drill.

```
The 14 boys, 9 girls and 1 adult had a picnic.          (9)
The lovely park was 49 miles from the town of 19,511.   (11)
Use firm, brisk strokes as you whiz through your ASA drills.  (12)
        2       4       6       8       10      12
```

TIMED WRITING

```
Speed range: 11 to 17 wpm
Error limit: 7 to 9
```

Do three, one-minute timed writings on the paragraphs below. Then do three, three-minute timed writings on the paragraphs. Complete the error correction drill immediately following each timed writing.

```
Five new members have been added to the 1989 reunion committee   (12)
of 41 members. We are asking one of them to please let us have a  (24)
report as soon as possible. Last year we took a wonderful         (35)
vacation cruise and we are eager to know what they have in store  (47)
for us this year. Although a lot of planning goes into our        (58)
annual get togethers, our group wants the early report because    (70)
we want to block any attempt to return to Happy Days Resort just  (82)
because it is only 78 miles from the city.                        (90)
    You will see that I have enclosed the names of the five new   (102)
committee members. Again it is my duty to rally the forces of     (114)
our group behind a luxury vacation like the one of 1990. That is  (126)
the reason for this letter. We believe we have presented our      (137)
case very well to the old members, but must now mount an all out  (149)
effort to make sure that the new members support our views.       (160)
Donald, that is where you come in. As in the past 10 years we     (171)
need your powerful influence behind our effort.                   (180)
        2       4       6       8       10      12
```

CHECKUP: Do not become overanxious about your errors, but try to keep them to a minimum. Remember to strike each key with equal force.

Master the drills above before proceeding to the next lesson. Use spare time to get extra practice.

Practice Session Ten

To develop speed, type smoothly, evenly, and continuously. Do not pause between strokes or at the end of a line. Be careful of slanting reaches. Keep your fingers curved, over the keys, wrists low. As you reach to the fourth key bank keep the other fingers in home key position.

NEW KEYS: 0 2 7 3 6

Strike the 0 key with your semicolon finger.

SEE IT, SAY IT, STRIKE IT

```
;0; ;0; ;0;
;0; ;0; ;0;
;0; ;0; ;0;
```

EYES ON THE COPY

```
;p; ;p; ;p0 ;p0 ;0p ;0p ;p; ;p; ;0; ;0; ;p01
10; .009 50; ;04 890 100 .01 .04 09; ;01 105
1095; popular 2590; March 10, 2,045 projects
```

The s-finger strikes the 2-key.

SEE IT, SAY IT, STRIKE IT

```
s2s s2s s2s
s2s s2s s2s
s2s s2s s2s
```

EYES ON THE COPY

```
sws sws s2s s2s sw2 sw2 2ws 2ws ws2 ws2 2w2w
2w2w 2s2s x2x2 s2s2 w2w2 x22w s22x w22s x2s2
22 was 209 are quantity .022; 259; 1922 town
```

Operate the 7-key with your j-finger.

SEE IT, SAY IT, STRIKE IT

```
j7j j7j j7j
j7j j7j j7j
j7j j7j j7j
```

EYES ON THE COPY

```
juj juj ju7 ju7 j7j j7j j7u j7u uj7 uj7 jum
jum jum7 jum7 muj7 muj7 789; jay 77 27; 007
77 days 47 Newark 7 and 8; 247 jets 107 777
```

Your d-finger will control the 3-key.

SEE IT, SAY IT, STRIKE IT

d3d d3d d3d
d3d d3d d3d
d3d d3d d3d

EYES ON THE COPY

ded ded d3d d3d de3 de3 3ed 3ed dcd dcd dc3
dc3 c3ed d3ec cde3 3edc d3d3 c3c3 e3e3 dc33
33 fellows 300 pigs 903 Fosters 3 golf tees

Use the j-finger to stroke the 6-key and you will complete the numbers'
row.

SEE IT, SAY IT, STRIKE IT

j6j j6j j6j
j6j j6j j6j
j6j j6j j6j

EYES ON THE COPY

juj juj ju6 ju6 jyj jyj jy6 jy6 6uj 6uj 6yj
6yj y6u y6u u6y u6y ujm6 uy6j mjy6 yum6 mj6
666 old 10, 657 Route 66 46 insureds 26,200

TECHNIQUE DEVELOPMENT

10 and 90; 20 and 99; 109 and .009; 409 and
The 5 employees drove 309 miles in one day.
we 23 24 25 we 23 22 21 it 85 86 87 it 85 8

the 27 first 77 vexed 107 sledge 7210; 7272
127-099 reviews 7089 acquits 2796 prizes 22
Ship it January 12, to 243 W. 277th Street.

we 33 yew 23 try 326 fun 032 riot 365 ewe 3
1962 highway 362 Main Street 630 puff 58630
Travel eastward on West 66th Street to see.

an 22 so 11 us 33 we 44 or 55 it 66 if 77 I
are wear read 609 more bear deer 483 done 1
pie 083 038 pie 380 038 pie 308 830 pie 803

The 23 boxes will arrive in the 1975 truck.
Buy all ten 1985 vans on the 10th of April.
A sale will be held on the 28th day of Feb.
Please order 10 of blue; 6 of red; at noon.

CHECKUP: Remember to read your text through completely before
typing it.

ACCURACY SPEED ACCURACY

As you complete the accuracy drills below try to type without an error. The goal of the first accuracy drill is to decrease your errors. On the speed drill go as fast as you can without losing control. On this segment of the drill you may pay more attention to speed than to control. The goal of the final accuracy drill is to put it all together, that is, to increase your speed without increasing your errors.

```
The 29 boxes were stored on the 7th floor on May 5th.      (10)
The brown foxes jumped over the 33 dogs who slept lazily.  (11)
One space follows a comma and a semicolon.                  (8)
         2        4        6        8       10       12
```

CHECKUP: Are you carefully following the instructions for the ASA drill and improving your accuracy and speed scores on each drill? Are you completing the entire drill (Accuracy Speed Accuracy) on each sentence before going on to the next as outlined on page 46? Are you completing the error correction drill following the first accuracy sentence? Review the instructions on pages 35–36 and repeat the drill above.

TIMED WRITING

```
Speed range: 11 to 18
Error limit: 6 to 9
```

Take three, one-minute timed writings followed by three, three-minute timed writings on the paragraphs below. Score and proofread carefully following each timing. Complete the error correction drill for any errors you make. If you are typing perfect copy, practice the reaches that were most difficult for you. Your accuracy goal is to type the entire timed writing without making an error and to increase your speed by five words. If you are making more than one error per minute you are probably out of control. Review the first few sessions and regain your control. FOLLOWING EACH TIMED WRITING IN WHICH YOU MAKE AN ERROR, COMPLETE THE ERROR CORRECTION DRILL.

```
Be rewarded with quick gain in your skill. If you wish to see      (12)
your speed rate go up and up, you must give the speed a big push   (24)
as you key these lines. Type the short words at high speeds,       (35)
like a race down hill.                                             (39)
     Give your speed a big push. Type at the new higher rate until (51)
you get the feel of the speed. Now you must move on to the next    (63)
step--keep the new speed for more and more time on more and more   (75)
lines.                                                             (76)
     If you use this idea each time you type you will build and    (87)
build your speed. Each time you get to a higher rate, hold on to   (99)
it. As you gain confidence on short words begin to work on       (110)
speeding right through long words too.                            (117)
     As you work to build your speed you will need to stay in     (128)
control. You will still need to keep your rate of making errors   (140)
very low. Your goal is to type at your fastest rate with few      (151)
```

errors. When you drill and drill your fingers until at last   (162)
they learn to make quick, easy, error free reaches, you grow.   (174)
    You will type at good rates when your typing has a steady   (185)
flow. When the copy is difficult drop to your slower pace but   (197)
speed up when the reaches are easy for you. The trick is not to   (209)
speed up or slow down too much.   (215)
    If you will give your speed a big push each time you type   (226)
these lines you will gain a big reward in your score. If you are   (238)
determined to follow the advice given here you will make your   (240)
goal.   (241)

        2   4   6   8   10   12

Master the drills above before proceeding to the next session.

Practice Session Eleven

In this session you will begin to learn the special characters of the standard typewriter keyboard. While the symbols themselves may appear unfamiliar to you, the reaches will not.

NEW KEYS: # $ % & ( ) Shift Lock ' !

   Perhaps you are wondering why there are so many new keys in one session. You have already had practice with most of the reaches, since the majority of the special characters are the upper case, or shift key position of your number keys.
   The # sign stands for the word "number" if it precedes a numeral. It stands for the word "pound," or "pounds" if it follows a numeral. DO NOT LEAVE SPACE BETWEEN THE # AND THE NUMERAL THAT PRECEDES OR FOLLOWS IT: #3, 7#. The # is controlled by the d-finger and the right shift.

SEE IT, SAY IT, STRIKE IT

d#d d#d d#d
d#d d#d d#d
d#d d#d d#d

EYES ON THE COPY

ded ded de3 de3 de# de# d#d d#d 3d# 3d# D#e D#e
Serial #9; Flight #347; birthday #100; 24#; 98#

Leave no space between the $ sign and the number that follows. The $ is controlled by the f-finger and the right shift.

SEE IT, SAY IT, STRIKE IT

f$f f$f f$f
f$f f$f f$f
f$f f$f f$f

EYES ON THE COPY

frf frf f4f f4f f$f f$f F$F F$F fr$ fr$ $4r f$F
$4.27; a bill for $209.21; and $6 now $2 for $1

Leave no space between the % sign and a number. The right shift key and your f-finger also control the % sign.

SEE IT, SAY IT, STRIKE IT

f%f f%f f%f
f%f f%f f%f
f%f f%f f%f

EYES ON THE COPY

ftf ftf f5f f5f f%f f%f F%F F%F ft% ft% %5 ftg%
25% .825% 20% discount charge 18% for 15% 100%

Leave a space before and after the ampersand (&). The &, which is the sign for "and," is controlled by your left shift and the j-finger.

SEE IT, SAY IT, STRIKE IT

```
j&j j&j j&j
j&j j&j j&j
j&j j&j j&j
```

EYES ON THE COPY

```
juj juj ju7 ju7 ju& ju& JU& JU& jm& jm& j&m 7&m
7&m j7&j j7&j ju&j ju&j Conklin & Cockrell & J&
```

Leave no space between the parentheses and the material they enclose. The left (is controlled by the l-finger and your left shift key.

SEE IT, SAY IT, STRIKE IT

```
l(l l(l l(l
l(l l(l l(l
l(l l(l l(l
```

EYES ON THE COPY

```
lol lol lo( lo( 19( 19( 9ol 9ol (9o (9o (ol (ol
lo(9 lo(9 .lo( .lo( 9. (o 9. (lo lo9( lo9( (ol. 9
```

The right) is controlled by the semicolon finger and the left shift.

SEE IT, SAY IT, STRIKE IT

```
;); ;); ;);
;); ;); ;);
;); ;); ;);
```

EYES ON THE COPY

```
;p; ;p; ;); ;); ;p) ;p) )p; p?) p?0 ;/) ;/) p0)
(1) (2) (3) (4) (5) (6) (7) (8) (9) (0) (10293)
```

Use the shift lock when you want to type a series of capital letters. To release the shift lock and return to small letters, strike the shift key. Use the a finger to depress the shift lock.

SEE IT, SAY IT, STRIKE IT

```
a lock A release a a lock A release a a lock A release a
aAa aAa aAa
aAa aAa aAa
```

EYES ON THE COPY

```
Use the shift lock to stress WORDS AND PHRASES.
SEE IT, SAY IT, STRIKE IT is the method she uses.
There is no space before or after an apostrophe within
a word. Use your semi finger to control the '.
```

SEE IT, SAY IT, STRIKE IT

```
;'; ;'; ;';
;'; ;'; ;';
;'; ;'; ;';
```

EYES ON THE COPY

```
;'; ;'; can't, don't, wouldn't, didn't, doesn't
I'll, Hers AMSTRADS' PCW8256's; Mildred's Ed's
```

Leave two spaces after an exclamation point at the end of a sentence, one space if within a sentence. Use your a finger and the right shift to control the !.

SEE IT, SAY IT, STRIKE IT

```
a!a a!a a!a
a!a a!a a!a
a!a a!a a!a
```

EYES ON THE COPY

```
aq! aq! qa! aq! qa! qa! It will! Help! Don't!
BOOM! Run! Run! Go team go! Never! Hurray!
```

TECHNIQUE DEVELOPMENT

```
Send my letter to him (the manager) via EXPRESS.
A total of 22# of the #3 lot were sold to Foley.
The price $188.00 was more than 25% of her cost.

The Dun & Bradstreet reports were very accurate.
The entire cost ($987.00) was paid by the owner.
Our new book GET RICH QUICK is the best buy yet!

Dole & Lark are featuring their Sip & Shake #27.
Our new company (Cole & Porter) deliver size #1.
PLEASE RUSH! Isn't he the one? Francis's play.
```

Complete the error correction drill.

ACCURACY SPEED ACCURACY

Complete an ASA drill on each of the sentences below. Do the error correction drill following the first accuracy drill.

```
Her friend (John) came to the #10 door.                    (8)
Vivian will agree to pay the entire bill! He shouted to Sam. (12)
Norwalk & Foster is the oldest firm in this city.          (10)
Their motto is repeated all over the area.                  (8)
        2        4        6        8       10       12
```

TIMED WRITING

Speed range: 12 to 19
Error limit: 6 to 8

Take three, one-minute timed writings on the very easy paragraph below. Try to type for the entire minute at your top speed without making a mistake. Complete the error correction drill between each timed writing.

It is a very good idea to try to practice every day when you are   (12)
learning a new skill like this one. Using a keyboard on a   (23)
computer is a fact of life today. It will save you time and   (34)
energy if you operate the computer keyboard by touch. So push   (46)
as hard as you can to master the keys. It may seem hard at first, (58)
but ease will come with practice. Try to be as accurate as you   (69)
can on the accuracy drill. Try to push for speed on the speed   (80)
drill until you gain that extra stroke. Set a goal and try to   (91)
make a little progress each day.   (97)
          2   4   6   8   10   12

Practice Session Twelve

When you complete this practice session you will have learned the special character keystrokes. This means you will have learned the entire standard typewriter keyboard. YOU ARE A TOUCH TYPIST.

As you type the lines below sit up straight, keep your wrists low and your elbows loosely at your sides.

NEW KEYS: backspace __ " * : = + ¢ ½ ¼ @
In this session you will also learn how to use the diagonal key to make fractions.

The backspace key is used to move the printing point or the cursor toward the left margin. DO NOT USE THE BACKSPACE KEY TO MAKE CORRECTIONS WHEN TYPING A DRILL. On the modern keyboard the backspace key (sometimes called the delete key) erases errors and allows the typist to insert correct material. In later sessions you will use this mechanism in your keyboard work; however, at this stage DO NOT CORRECT ERRORS in this fashion. People who do so run the risk of placing a permanently low ceiling on their speed. They also run the risk of never really gaining control over accuracy. Use these sessions to build skill by following the instructions for the error correction drills at the end of each technique development and timed writing sections.

CHECKUP: Are you relaxed? Did you complete the foundation exercise? Are you striking and releasing the keys like they are hot? Remember, when your mind wanders, entice it right back. If it continues to do so, take a short break of a minute or two and regain your control.

SEE IT, SAY IT, STRIKE IT

```
;backspace; ;backspace; ;backspace;
;backspace; ;backspace; ;backspace;
;backspace; ;backspace; ;backspace;
```

Titles of books, films, television shows, plays, and record albums are underlined. You may underline any word you wish to appear in italics. Many modern, electronic keyboards provide a special code key for typing the underline. Check your manual. If you are using a special code key the underscoring may occur simultaneously with your keystroking. Follow the directions in your manual. Otherwise, the underline key is the shift of the hyphen. If the underline on your keyboard is not operated by a special code key, use the shift lock when you wish to underscore a series of letters or words. First type the letters or words you wish to underscore. Then use the backspace key to return to the first letter by backspacing. Use the semicolon finger and the left shift to control the underscore key.

SEE IT, SAY IT, STRIKE IT

;_; ;_; ;_;
;_; ;_; ;_;
;_; ;_; ;_;

EYES ON THE COPY

The New York Times is often read by many people.
Parting the Waters--by Taylor Branch--sells out.

The asterisk is used to signal attention or note. Leave no space between the asterisk and the word it appears before or after. Use the left shift and your k-finger to control the *.

SEE IT, SAY IT, STRIKE IT

k*k k*k k*k
k*k k*k k*k
k*k k*k k*k

EYES ON THE COPY

kik kik K8k k*k ki* ki* k8* k8* *ilk *ilk* *ill*

Use the asterisk (*) sign for reference. *3318#

Leave no space between quotation marks and the material they enclose. The quotation is the shift of the apostrophe. Use the semi finger and left shift to control it.

SEE IT, SAY IT, STRIKE IT

;"; ;"; ;";
;"; ;"; ;";
;"; ;"; ;";

EYES ON THE COPY

;"; ;"; ;'; ;'; """ """ "It is, you'll "see!" '
"Give it to them," was her command to the teams.

Leave a space on either side of both the plus sign and the equal sign. Use the semicolon finger and your left shift.

SEE IT, SAY IT, STRIKE IT

;=; ;+; ;=;
;=; ;+; ;=;
;=; ;+; ;=;

EYES ON THE COPY

:=; :=; ;+; ;+; 9 + 11 = 20; 4 + 7 + 4 + 3 = 18;
Y = X, A = L + C is basic to good accounting. +

Leave no space before and after the signs ½, ¼. Leave one space after the ½, ¼ signs when a word follows. The ½ is controlled by the semi finger. The ¼ is the shift of the ½.

SEE IT, SAY IT, STRIKE IT

; ½ ; ; ¼ ; ; ½ ;
; ½ ; ; ¼ ; ; ½ ;
; ½ ; ; ¼ ; ; ½ ;

EYES ON THE COPY

; ½ ; ; ½ ; ; ¼ ; ; ¼ ; 10 ½ #; ship 12 ¼ 8 ½ 6 ¼ 5 ½ %
She used 24 ½ gallons of gasoline for the drives.

When you want to keystroke a fraction other than the ½ or ¼ use the diagonal key: 5/8 3/4 7/10. When a fraction made with a diagonal is preceded by a number leave a space between the number and the fraction: 22 3/10; 49 6/7.

Leave no space between a number and the ¢ sign. Use the j-finger and the left shift to control the ¢ sign.

SEE IT, SAY IT, STRIKE IT

j¢j j¢j j¢j
j¢j j¢j j¢j
j¢j j¢j j¢j

EYES ON THE COPY

j¢j j¢j j&j j&j j¢& J&¢ 67j j67 67¢ 67¢ & 76¢ J¢
1¢ 2¢ 3¢ 4¢ 55¢ 66¢ 77¢ 88¢ 99¢ 11¢ 22¢ 33¢ +44¢

Leave a space before and after the @ sign. Use the s-finger and the right shift key to control the @ sign.

SEE IT, SAY IT, STRIKE IT

s@s s@s s@s
s@s s@s s@s
s@s s@s s@s

EYES ON THE COPY

sws sws s@s s@s s2s s2s s@s s@s 22 @ cost 90 @ ½
The sign @ is used to bill--900# @ $1000.00 per.

TECHNIQUE DEVELOPMENT

In southern California the weather is very good.
"Please come to the #2 lot." He wrote for her.*
Dear James: Inches: 10:00 S + M = SM: Dear Sir:

The shelf is between ½ and ¼ inches too short.
Send her 25% of the package @ $240.00 per dozen.
Batman is a very popular movie on Foster street.

For 8 days she awaited his arrival from the sea.
*See below for more information. **August 19th.
The quotations were as follows: 3 @ $9; 7 @ $4.

Complete the error correction drill.

ACCURACY SPEED ACCURACY

The whole unit is just 24 feet high.   (7)
<u>Underscored</u> words are given triple value in the word count.   (12)
"Tonight! Tonight!" The cheerleaders shouted.   (9)
         2   4   6   8   10   12

TIMED WRITING

Speed range: 13 to 20
Error range: 5 to 7

Take three, one-minute timed writings on the easy material below. Use
this very easy paragraph to build your speed and accuracy.

We need your help. We wish to make a study to find   (8)
out the kinds of automobiles that people in this state want and (18)
need. With so many at work now, we feel we must keep in close (27)
touch with you so that we can give you all the help that we (36)
can at a cost that you can afford to pay. Will you please   (45)
read and check the list of questions you find on this form? (54)
You can help us a great deal to help you with the right auto. (63)
This will mean a great deal to you, so please check your   (72)
answers now and return them.   (76)
         2   4   6   8   10

CHECKUP: Did you complete the error correction drill according to
instructions? When you are typing drill lines remember to double-space
after each pair of lines. Always read your text through completely before
keyboarding it.

Practice Session Thirteen

Use this session to build your skill and refine your technique. Do the error correction drill at the end of each section of drill lines. Strive to master the reaches, keystroking each line without error. Keep your wrists low. Try to type short words as a whole instead of letter by letter. Think or say the word; type it. Master the lines below before going on to the next session.

SKILL DEVELOPMENT

```
ear; rear hear fear ear; dear told sold fold mold
dell sell jell fell tall all; fall hall all; dell
lock came dock colt chat call dice come hock rich

Verse Vera very vast various travel save Savoy Vi
havoc herd Hallie Hannah harm hope host hostile H
their those they that this the there therefore th

If if we do if we go if we can if we came if I if
illegal diffuse muddles allow called affect alloy
argued flower lucent lucky older answer juicy oil

juvenile poetry educate bacon recipe carton shine
lesson Phoenix museum muster swaying lawyer awake
seized rivals reveal scenic yawn burden enable in
```

Complete the error correction drill.

CHECKUP: Are you typing each line twice and double-spacing between the pairs by striking the return key twice at the end of the second line?

NUMBERS AND SPECIAL CHARACTERS

```
aqla ;p0; sw2s lo9l de3d ki8k de3d ju7j fr4f hy6j
fr5f fr4f ki8* (99) 1839 234% "12" 67 + 10 = 77**
The thirty (30) young ladies carried a 9# parcel.

aggravate $234.00 excavate 57% homonym 99¢ Means:
up 80 quip 570 yore 9842 tight 61659 box 935 poet
writ 5500 poor 5909 purr 4761 quay 9495 putty 758

fr4f fr$f f$f F$F $4 $4 $4.00 ;/; ;/; 1 1/3 4 34½
;-; ;-; 6-cent 78-31 1919 1(1 ;0; );); (p) ;'; ;';
de3d de3# de3# De#D De#d #78* don't 72 @ 5% + 15¢
```

```
How could 81 boys and 99 women use up 999 tickets?
I hired 576 full-time workers and 27 part-timers.
WHOLESALE PRICES! (Crest Cleaners) 3621 Broadway
```

Complete the error correction drill.

REACHES

12:00 p.m. Dear Mr. Phillips: I am at the Woods.
island excitement ordeal kidney vacant active eat
sequel unpack reveal flexed Mexico versus avenues

crazily Malaysia handling cycled antique chickens
jackets wigwams excessive aquarium Victory gloats
vaccine folklore zoomed frequently vegetables day

expressions penalized qualified bribery encore an
deeded daunt Donald plump equity enlist tattoo Van
unequal ukuleles unjust zipper yacht crew renewed
allowed welcome dropped tastily street hearts add

Complete the error correction drill.

PARAGRAPHS

Type each of the paragraphs below twice. Try to keystroke at your top
speed without making an error.

The #2 train will arrive on track #4 at 2:00 p.m.
tomorrow. Mary will meet Jim and me there.

    The great pot of beans was stewing on the stove.
The aroma coming from the big black pot was a good welcome
for hungry travelers.

I invested $10,000 in the Cash Dividend (CD) account at
EUROPEAN AMERICAN BANK. The interest rate was a high 15.5% (not
the low 9.89% of most other banks in this area).

    It is a good idea for the typist to know the basic rules of
English: For instance, the closing quotation mark is typed
after a period or comma, but it is typed before a colon or
semicolon. ALWAYS!

Complete the error correction drill.

CHECKUP: Did you complete the error correction drill following each
section above? Make reaches between bottom and top rows without
stopping on the home keys. Type evenly and smoothly.

ACCURACY SPEED ACCURACY

```
The good-looking woman calmly made the speech.        (9)
It has become too costly, so we charge a fee.         (9)
Rex & Sons sent us Invoice #31 for $70.82 yesterday. (10)
If they haven't, please give them a call.             (8)
Please do so as soon as you get back from the meeting. (11)
        2       4       6       8      10      12
```

TIMED WRITING

Speed range: 14 to 21
Error range: 5 to 7

Take three, one-minute and three, three-minute timed writings on the paragraph below. ALWAYS COMPLETE THE ERROR CORRECTION DRILL BETWEEN EACH TIMED WRITING.

```
Everyone should learn how to type. It is a skill that all can    (11)
use throughout life. You do not have to type to earn money for   (23)
typing to be a useful skill. Just knowing how to type will make  (35)
your life easier. Being able to type will save you time and      (46)
effort. And, since typing produces cleaner text you should       (57)
always think of typing rather than writing. It is much faster,   (69)
you know.                                                        (71)
    There are many ways you can use typing personally. You can   (83)
type letters to friends, government agencies, and people in      (94)
business. If you are a student, your teachers will be very      (105)
happy to get neatly typed copy from you. Did you know that      (116)
studies show that students who type their papers get higher     (127)
grades than those who do not?                                   (133)
    Even if you do not want to make money typing, it is a skill  (145)
that is always in demand.                                       (150)
        2       4       6       8      10      12
```

Push for new levels of speed and accuracy with each session of practice. Practice! Practice! Practice! Remember, practice is not just the way to get to Carnegie Hall; it is also a way to develop that efficient typist who can always be assured of finding work. As you try to gain speed type steadily, continuously, not hurriedly. Be a master of the drills above before proceeding.

Practice Session Fourteen

Practice the skill-building lines below and complete the error correction drill. Then type the drill a second time. Strive to type each line through twice at your top speed without making an error.
Type each line twice double-spacing between the pairs.

```
the no so of there their there to very and other
in should you no information we office yours now
year your more that me is enclosed some this has


business we service company were have our out if
about I know as up company them which copy would
please appreciate made an each only about letter
```

HORIZONTAL AND VERTICAL CENTERING

There will be times when you will wish to arrange your material attractively on the page. One way to accomplish attractive layouts is by centering.

Horizontal Centering

When you set your margin you are accomplishing horizontal centering. What you will learn here is how to center shorter lines without adjusting your margin stops. Word processors have an automatic centering feature that allows you to center a line or group of lines without backspacing. If you are not using a word processor, center words across the page in this manner:

1. Set the printing point at the center point of the paper: 42 for pica and 50 for elite.
2. Backspace from the center once for every two characters and/or spaces on the line. (When you backspace in this way you are actually dividing by two.)
3. Say the strokes (including spaces) to yourself in pairs, pressing and releasing the backspace key one time for each pair of strokes. If you have a character left over do not backspace for this letter.
4. Type the words.

Practice the lines below:

```
You are Invited
to a Spring Festival
Saturday, May 14th
3:00 p.m. until!
Harlem YMCA
3779 West 135th Street
```

CHECKUP: Do your lines look like this?

<pre>
                    You Are Invited

                  to a Spring Festival

                  Saturday, May 14th

                  3:00 p.m. until!

                     Harlem YMCA

                3779 West 135th Street
</pre>

Vertical Centering

For material to appear attractively on the page it is important for the top and bottom margins to appear to be the same. You accomplish this by centering vertically. On most typewriters and word processors 6 lines equal an inch. Standard typing paper is 11 inches long or 66 lines. A half sheet is 33 lines deep. To center a group of lines and provide for an equal top and bottom margin:

1. Count the lines—blank ones too—the material will occupy when typed.
2. Subtract the number from 66.
3. Divide the remainder by 2 dropping any fractions.
4. Using the number you just arrived at, count down the number of lines from the top of the page. Begin typing your copy here.

There are 11 lines in the material above: $66 - 11 = 55 \div 2 = 27$. If you are using a full sheet of paper you will begin typing on line 27. Center the material above on a full sheet of paper. Then center the same material on a half sheet of paper.

Block Centering

To center a block of material find the longest line in the copy. From the center of the page backspace once for every two letters or spaces in that line. Set your left margin at the point where you stopped backspacing.

Practice the lines below:

<pre>
TROUBLESOME SPELLING WORDS
Amortize
Hypocrisy
Beneficiaries
Chronological
Presumptuously
Psychologically
</pre>

CHECKUP: Do your lines look like this?

```
        TROUBLESOME SPELLING WORDS
        Amortize
        Hypocrisy
        Beneficiaries
        Chronological
        Presumptuously
        Psychologically
```

Now center this material vertically.

TABULATION OR FORMATTING A TABLE

Sometimes you will want to organize your text in the form of a table. The basic parts of a table are:

1. TITLE: Identifies the contents of the table. Center and type in all-capital letters.
2. SUBTITLE: Gives further information about the table. Center and double-space below the title with the first and all principal words capitalized.
3. COLUMN HEADING: Tells what is in each column. Center over the column and underscore; leave 2 blank lines before and 1 blank line after.
4. BODY: Center the columns horizontally, usually with 6 blank spaces between columns; depending upon the length of the table you may single- or double-space the material.

Planning the Table Format

1. Move the margins to the extreme left and right. Clear out all tab stops.
2. SELECT THE KEY LINE. This is the longest item in each column, plus 6 blank spaces for each open area between columns.
3. SET LEFT MARGIN. From the center of the paper backspace once for every two spaces or characters in the key line and set the left margin at the point to which you have backspaced. DO NOT BACKSPACE FOR AN EXTRA STROKE.
4. SET TAB STOPS. From the left margin, space forward across the paper once for each letter and each space in the longest item of the first column, plus 6 blank spaces, and set a tab stop. From the first tab stop, space forward for each letter and each space in the longest item in the second column, plus 6 blank spaces, and set the second tab stop. Space forward from the second tab stop for each letter and each space, plus 6 blank spaces, and set the third tab stop. Continue in this manner until you have set tabs for all columns in the table.
5. CENTER VERTICALLY. Subtract the number of lines in the table from the length of your paper and divide by 2. This is the line you will place your heading on.
6. Backspace-center the title, and type it in all caps.

7. Type the subheading a double-space below the title. Backspace-center the subheading.
8. Always type columns across the page using the tabulator key to move from column to column.

Practice the short table below:

OFFICE WORKERS

Rosalind A. Howard	Receptionist
Betty Jones	Typist
Ralph Smith	Clerk
Vera Williams	Typist
Sue Ray	Secretary

Center the three-column table below horizontally and vertically:

TOP BRANCH MANAGERS
ESTIMATED SALARIES AND DEPARTMENTS

Delores Lewis	Frames	$36,000
Donald Bogle	Shoes	$35,000
Josephus Ray Robinson	Photographs	$27,500.22
Carla Bush	Utensils	$22,000.59

Column headings will help your reader understand the information presented. Block the heading over the column by keeping the heading and column entries flush left. If the column heading is the longest line in the column, use it to calculate the tab stop. Practice the table below.

FAMOUS AMERICAN ATHLETES

Player	Sport	Team
Babe Ruth	Baseball	New York Yankees
Jesse Owens	Track	1936 Olympics
Kareem Abdul-Jabbar	Basketball	Los Angeles Lakers

Practice Session Fifteen

As you practice the skill-building lines below do not think speed, think smooth. Try to type smoothly without error at your top speed. Set a brisk pace on short words and maintain it on longer words. Type each line twice double-spacing between. Complete the error correction drill following each section.

SKILL BUILDING

inn see ill boo egg too tee zoo err odd all a
bee err tall toll putt miss bill boss buff do
less pass well knee mill foll will hood foods

alerts solemn safer artery avoids blown diode
trade radius biopsy sedans medium either lien
movie incurs biased surer alumni ascent peeks

ghetto unmask dirty mystic divide words often
adhere artery idiot oldest suing lights track
cliff funny breed robber accord agreed accept

myopia cupful inroad wrote youth reader blade
bounce course sofa gasses garage behind dance
affair abbey cabbage express fillet seeks old

Complete the error correction drill and retype the lines in which the errors occurred.

NUMBERS AND SYMBOLS

9301 5902 2803 7604 9805 3506 4907 9908 3409%
6710 4511 8412 5813 6614 3015 4016 2017 8118#
6819 8920 1921 1722 4623 9624 1625 3526 4417*

acre 457 crew 901 trio 345 diet 676 void 280+
them 555 they 515 turn 777 down 666 town 010=
$5.00 $6.00 $7.00 $8.00 $9.00 $2.15 $8.90 $10

The 22 bright young girls ran 55 miles today.
Sean's expensive gift ($199.99) is beautiful.
Rhonda will arrive on July 7, at gate #6788A.

PARAGRAPHS

You can improve both your speed and your accuracy by developing better typing techniques. For example, by always returning the carrier without looking up you avoid the time wasted when you have to find your place in the copy. Always use the tabulator key to indent your paragraphs. Set your machine for double-space as you type each paragraph below through twice. After you type the paragraph through the first time, proofread it to find all of your mistypes and complete the error correction drill. The second time try to type the paragraph without error. Remember a quick, smooth carrier return adds to your typing speed. Type the paragraphs below.

Indeed, inputs, infers, inform, inches and indent, are all words that begin with "in." But input is the only one that refers directly to computers.

Thomas Jefferson served as President of the United States of America from 1801 to 1809. John Adams served as president from 1797 to 1801. He died on Independence Day (July 4th) in 1826 at the ripe old age of 90.

Mrs. Zackery always paid her rent on time. On May 27th she got a notice from her landlord saying her rent was past due. But Mrs. Zackery was not worried. She had her cancelled check #4670 for $345.98, the full amount of her rent.

In the past only clerical workers needed typing skills. In the modern office of today managers need the ability to type accurately just as much as do clerical workers. Many managers in today's business office have small computers on their desks. Many homes are now equipped with computers. In today's world it is important for everyone to realize that he or she will need to know how to TYPE BY TOUCH!

CHECKUP: Did you complete the error correction before the second keyboarding of each paragraph?

ACCURACY SPEED ACCURACY

We have acknowledged the receipt of their order.   (10)
To type at high speeds, keep your arms almost motionless.   (12)
When typing, keep your fingers curved rather than straight.   (12)
          2   4   6   8   10   12

TIMED WRITING

Take three, one-minute timed writings and three, three-minute timed writings on the easy text below. Remember to complete the error correction drill between each timing.

Speed range: 15 to 21
Error range: 5 to 7

Each time you type a drill line you want to try to do it better   (12)
than the time before. You do not want to repeat your mistakes.   (24)
Each time you do a drill you want to really try to do it in a   (35)
better way than the time before. Be critical, and size up your   (47)
problems with a goal of learning better methods of increasing   (59)
speed and accuracy.   (63)

For example, an important point to remember when you type   (74)
numbers or symbols is to type them accurately and to type   (85)
without looking at the keyboard. Avoid glancing down at the   (96)
keys each time. As you learn to concentrate on accuracy and   (107)
technique your skill is assured.   (113)

Another important point to remember is not to pause at the   (125)
end of a line before making the return. Strike the return key as (137)
soon as you type the last stroke in the line. Make the return   (148)
with quick motions and begin the new line with almost no pause. (160)
Keeping your eyes on the copy as you make the return is a very   (171)
important point of technique. When you make your return   (182)
quickly and smoothly, without looking away from your copy your (194)
speed is bound to increase.   (199)

    2   4   6   8   10   12

CHECKUP: Are you reading the text before you begin keyboarding it? A good typist understands what she or he is about to input. Did you complete the error correction drill for the ASA drill and the TIMED WRITING?

If you are typing at a rate higher than the speed range and with fewer errors than the error range, that is excellent! If your score is below the range for speed and above the range for errors, review the earlier sessions and continue to practice diligently. Some people get off to a very fast start while others get off to a slower start. With consistent, dedicated practice you can become a good typist. Remember not to go on to the next session until you have mastered the previous one.

Practice Session Sixteen

In the previous session you have been occupied with learning the keyboard and building speed and accuracy. In this session the emphasis is on learning how to correct your errors when you are typing correspondence that will be transmitted to others. You will also learn the basic forms of personal and business communications. Although you will learn how to correct errors, you will use this technique only when typing correspondence to be transmitted to others. DO NOT CORRECT ERRORS WHEN TYPING THE DRILLS DESIGNED TO BUILD SPEED AND ACCURACY. USE THE ERROR CORRECTION DRILL.

ERROR CORRECTION

Whether you are typing for money or for your personal use, you must NEVER SEND COPY THAT CONTAINS ERRORS. Review the definition of an error on page 35. All typists make errors at one time or another; therefore, it is important to know how to correct your mistypes. Of course the very first step is the ability to proofread carefully before printing or removing the hard copy from the machine. Many times you will know as soon as you make a mistake that an error has occurred. STOP IMMEDIATELY AND CORRECT IT.

When you are typing copy that will be transmitted to others it is best to stop after every one or two paragraphs to proofread what you have recorded. To correct an error when typing on a word processor or computer, delete the incorrect letters and retype the correct ones.

The vast majority of modern typewriters are self-correcting, that is, they are outfitted with a correction ribbon. This ribbon is operated by a special backspace key. Use this special backspace key to return to the error and then retype the error. The thin layer of white chalk on the ribbon will cover the error. Now type in the correction. On the latest models as you backspace, the characters you have just typed are removed. In this way the special backspace key leaves clean white space for you to retype the correction.

If your typewriter is not self-correcting use correction paper. It can be purchased at most office supply stores. Backspace to the error and place the slip of paper containing a light coating of chalk between the typing paper and the typewriter ribbon with the coated side toward the paper. Retype the error. The chalk will cover the mistype so that you can now retype the correct character. Remove the correction paper, backspace, and type the correction.

The goal of the typist is to always present the best possible image in her or his typewritten work. Therefore, it is critical to develop error correcting techniques that are not detectable. Avoid starting over, it is a waste of time and energy. Learn to find and correct your errors so that they are undetectable!

Use the method appropriate to your keyboard to correct errors on the following drills.

BUSINESS LETTERS

The basic parts of a business letter are:

1. LETTERHEAD: Printed name and address of the company. Usually appears at the head of the stationery.
2. DATELINE: Month, day, and year the letter is typed.
3. INSIDE ADDRESS: Name and address of the party to whom you are writing.
4. SALUTATION: Opening greeting.
5. BODY: Message or text of the letter.
6. COMPLIMENTARY CLOSING: Closing farewell.
7. SIGNATURE LINE: Handwritten signature of the writer.
8. WRITER'S IDENTIFICATION: Typed name and title of the writer.
9. REFERENCE SYMBOLS: Initials of the typist and the dictator of the letter.
10. ENCLOSURE NOTATION: Notifies addressee of attachments.

Whether you are typing a business letter or a personal business letter you will want the text to appear attractively on the page. Arrange your letters on the page to give the impression of a picture in a frame. Use the placement information below to determine margin settings and the line on which to type the date of the letter.

Letter Placement

1. Short: up to 100 words use a 40-space line of pica type or 50-space line of elite type. Type the date on line 20.
2. Average: 101 to 200 words use a 50-space line of pica type or a 60-space line of elite type. Type the date on line 15–18 depending upon the length of the letter.
3. Long: 201 to 300 words use a 60-space pica line and a 70-space elite line of type. Type the date on line 13.
4. 2-page: 300+ words use a 60-space pica line of type or a 70-space elite line of type. Type the date on line 13.

The word count is provided for you on the letters that follow. Use the chart above to format these letters.

An important ingredient in formatting your business letters is choosing a style. There are several business letter styles. You will learn the most commonly used ones here.

Modified Block Style:

This is the most commonly used business letter style. Business letters in the modified block style begin the date and closing lines at the center of the page. All other lines begin at the left margin. The paragraphs may or may not be indented. Business letters are always single-spaced unless the letter is a very short one of two or three lines of type.

Full Block:

This is the second most often used style of business letter. In the full block style all lines begin at the left margin.

Personal Letters

When typing the personal letter you will need to include your return address, unless you have printed letterhead stationery. While the personal letter is written to a friend, relative, or acquaintance, about personal matters, the personal business letter is written by an individual to a company or organization about business matters. As with the personal letter if you do not have stationery with your printed address you will need to type in your return address. Type the personal business letter below. It appears in modified block style without paragraph indention.

5929 Greene Street	(4)
Topeka, KS 66606	(8)
December 21, 19	(10)

Space down 4 times

Mr. Carl Reed	(12)
Air Waves Inc.	(15)
3000 Woodward Avenue	(19)
Detroit, MI 48204	(23)

  DS

Dear Mr. Reed:	(26)

DS

When your saleswoman visited our home on July 22nd she told us	(38)
that your plan would give us the best service in town. She said	(50)
that if we would agree to spend a few dollars more we would get	(62)
regular visits from your service people to check the system.	(74)

We are very sorry to tell you that the young man who visited our	(86)
home last week to examine the central heating and	(95)
air-conditioning system was very rude. The furnace has worked	(107)
very well. We like it very much. We also think your saleslady	(118)
was right to sell us the service plan. However, we do not want	(129)

Howard Kemp to make the service calls. In the future please   (140)
send someone to our home who is pleasant and courteous.   (150)
     DS

                         Sincerely yours,   (153)

                         Space down 4 times

                         Alexis P. Johnson   (156)

     Since Alexis P. Johnson typed the above letter herself there is no
need for reference symbols.
     If a letter is addressed to a company rather than to an individual
the appropriate salutation is Ladies and Gentlemen. Type the letter
above a second time. This time use the following inside address and
salutation:

Air Waves Incorporated
Service Department
3000 Woodward Avenue
Detroit, MI 48204

Ladies and Gentlemen:

Repeat the drills in this session until you have mastered them.

Practice Session Seventeen

BUSINESS LETTERS AND INTEROFFICE MEMORANDA

Type each of the letters below, correcting your errors using the error correction technique described in the previous session. Although it is not necessary to type your reference symbols on letters you type for yourself, you will include them on letters you type for others. Remember the reference symbols are the initials of the typist and the person who wrote the letter. The business letter below is formatted in the modified block style with paragraph indention.

Doer & Donne
Public Relations Consultants
2 Wilshire Boulevard
Los Angeles, CA 90242

September 27, 19   (4)
Space down 4 times

Mrs. Bette Lou Irving   (9)
555 Northwest Outer Drive   (15)
Brooklyn, NY 11210   (19)
DS
Dear Mrs. Irving: (23)
  DS
   May I ask you a personal question? When you look in the   (34)
mirror, is your skin as smooth, as soft, and as young-looking (46)
as you'd like it to be? If you feel that it is not, please do not (58)
fault your skin. It just might be that the culprit is sitting (69)
right there in your soap dish! Your soap can leave your skin   (80)
dull and grey.   (83)

   Women in the know now use LOVE. Love is not a soap. It is a   (94)
mild gentle cleansing foam that is one-half cold cream. While (105)
Love foams below the surface and cleans deeply in your pores it (117)
does not dry and irritate your skin like soap. It restores your (129)
skin, leaving it soft and smooth.   (135)

Try Love today and see what a beautiful difference it will   (146)
make in your complexion.   (151)
   DS

                    Sincerely,   (153)

                    space down 4 times

                    Shirley Campbell   (156)
                    Marketing Manager   (160)
   DS
rb/sc
Enc.: Free Sample   (165)

Memoranda

An interoffice memorandum (memo) is a letter from one employee to another in the same organization. It may be typed on a special memorandum form, on plain paper, or on letterhead. When typing interoffice correspondence the salutation and complimentary closing are omitted.

Formatting Interoffice Memoranda

1. Begin typing the heading on line 7 when using a half sheet of paper and on line 13 of a full sheet of paper.
2. Set a 10-space tab stop to align the heading information.
3. Use a 5-inch line (50 pica/60 elite).
4. Leave 2 blank lines between the heading and the body of the memorandum.
5. Include your reference initials.

Keyboard the interoffice correspondence below correcting all of your errors.

TO: All Secretaries and Typists

FROM: Jason Watson, Personnel Manager

Date: February 22, 19

SUBJECT: Proofreading Tips

Recently many executives and managers have complained of letters and reports leaving the office with a large number of typographical errors. Please use the following proofreading tips for all correspondence.

Read each letter through twice. The first time read for content and logic. The second time read for mistypes. As you read the letter check all numbers, proper names, and addresses. Watch for often confused words such as capital and capitol, effect and affect, except and accept. Check all of the letter parts, not just the material in the body.

When proofreading on a VDT (video display tube) or CRT (cathode
ray tube) it is best to scroll the material line by line from
the beginning. You may use your software dictionary to check
the spelling of words.

lg/jw

The full block style is the second most often used business letter format.
Type the full block letter below, correcting all of your errors. Review
previous letters. Leave the appropriate number of spaces between the
letter parts.

Computer Solutions, Inc.

2020 Main Street
Detroit, Michigan 48080

(313) 888-1234

March 14, 19   (5)

Samantha Dunn, Editor-In-Chief   (11)
FOR THE MODERN WOMAN   (16)
78 Bayside Drive   (19)
San Francisco, CA 94109   (24)

Dear Ms. Dunn: (27)

Thank you for your inquiry about the use of word processing in   (39)
your office. We have looked very closely at your needs and see   (51)
that your office will get fine results from a wide range of   (62)
models.   (64)

For example, some word processors have a column-layout feature   (76)
that automatically aligns column headings. Nearly all of them   (88)
will allow you to insert and delete a unit of text   (98)
automatically.   (101)

Information that is sent to a word processing department is   (112)
called input. Since the original text or input is stored on a   (124)
tape or disk when you wish to make revisions only the changed   (136)
material must be retyped.   (141)

Ms. Dunn, we can share much more information with you if you   (152)
will please call our office to arrange a conference.   (162)

Sincerely yours,   (165)

Robert A. Johnson   (169)
Information Processing Specialist   (176)

op/raj   (177)

CHECKUP: How does your letter look on the page? Does it look like a beautiful picture in a frame with equal margins surrounding it? Be careful not to place your letter too high or too low on the page.

Repeat all of the drills in this session until you have mastered them.

PART TWO:
Skill Building

In Part One you learned the entire letter, number, and special character keyboard, and the proper techniques for striking the keys. You also learned the most commonly used forms of basic business correspondence. In the sessions to follow you will concentrate on building your skill, on improving your speed and accuracy. You will do this by concentrating on proper technique.

CHECKUP: Before going any further it is time for a thorough self-evaluation. Is your keystroking technique under control? Are you making steady progress? Do you know the entire standard-typewriter keyboard by memory? Are you a touch typist?

Your fingers cannot fly over the keyboard if you do not know where the keys are. If you do not know the keyboard by memory, go back to the beginning lessons and learn it. If you do know the keyboard by memory but get out of control on the speed drills, begin to work at a comfortable, rhythmic pace until you gain control. Remember, typewriting is brain work too. Your speed will build proportionately to the amount of thought you apply to it. Typing drills can be fun if you become a part of the process and experience the challenge and inspiration. Beware of reducing your keyboarding skill to a mere motor activity. It is far more than that.

Throughout the practice keep checking on your motions. It only takes one or two bad habits to cut your speed down. The worst of these, and perhaps the most common too, is not keeping your eyes on the copy. When you put too much arm and hand motion in your keystroking, you impede your speed gain and tire more easily. Good stroking requires curved, properly aligned fingers, quiet arms and hands, and most important of all, CONCENTRATION. Remember you want to train your fingers to follow the same correct path from keystroke to keystroke, and to accomplish this your posture is critical.

Follow standard instructions as you key the lines below.

EASY WORDS

ask you are for was may wed the you rug cap aid got air get
oil ill the man due them is ever on hand to join if only as
bust best the hand so there of their very to other in where

should enclosed will now would thank you made every only at
during copy people account forward them from some few about

life circumstances opportunity interested due might schools
type and building property before after special course fear
advise advice hope must sure which that hospital paid total

Complete the error correction drill.

ALTERNATING FINGERS

above options bound diem eschew influx friend company happy
element penalty exceeds because engulf loom title cycle due
focus thematic strategy when request complete forwarded see

best application concerning necessary both manner sedans do
coined loans reason errors prior avoids auditor eleven free
theirs wrong prerequisite personnel invoice escaped enigmas

Complete the error correction drill.

COMMON PHRASES

Master the following phrases at optimal speed and accuracy.

it is it is as it is as if it is as if the it as if she its
with both; with them; at all, date due, by the way: can he

HIGH RISK COMBINATIONS

i/o
boil oil soil coil avoid intolerant objective biology polio
outline foil folio iron coiled environments inclusion broil
portfolio spoils suggestion invention constitution invoices

TIMED WRITING

Take three, one-minute timed writings and three, five-minute timed
writings on the material below. Remember to complete the error correction drill between each timed writing. Practice the preview lines and
correct your errors before beginning the timed writings.

Speed Range: 18 to 26+
Error range: 5 to 6

PREVIEW

Realistic critical important productive enough challenge   (11)
experience blindly through struggle deficiencies stronger   (22)
motivate practice so   (26)

Realistic goal setting is critical to good life planning. It is (38)
also very important for building typing skill. The best   (49)
typists, like the most productive, set daily goals. They are (61)
careful not to set their goals too high. Yet, they want enough (73)
challenge so that each experience is a growing one. We grow in (85)
skill, day by day, little by little. You cannot plod along   (96)

blindly through your day's work and hope to make progress. Each (108)
day as you struggle to achieve your goals you will be alert to   (119)
your deficiencies. Remedy them and grow.   (127)
     2   4   6   8   10   12

TABULATION REVIEW

Center vertically and horizontally and tabulate this table of two-letter state abbreviations. Proofread carefully correcting all errors. Save, post, learn, and use these abbreviations for all of your domestic mail.

TWO-LETTER STATE ABBREVIATIONS

Alabama	AL	Montana	MT
Alaska	AK	Nebraska	NE
Arizona	AZ	Nevada	NV
Arkansas	AR	New Hampshire	NH
District of Columbia	DC	North Dakota	ND
Florida	FL	Ohio	OH
Georgia	GA	Oklahoma	OK
Hawaii	HI	Oregon	OR
Idaho	ID	Pennsylvania	PA
Illinois	IL	Puerto Rico	PR
Indiana	IN	Rhode Island	RI
Iowa	IA	South Carolina	SC
Kansas	KS	South Dakota	SD
Kentucky	KY	Tennessee	TN
Louisiana	LA	Texas	TX
Maine	ME	Utah	UT
Maryland	MD	Vermont	VT
Massachusetts	MA	Virginia	VA
Michigan	MI	Wisconsin	WI
Missouri	MO	Wyoming	WY

Practice Session Eighteen

The following practice sessions will contain fewer and fewer drill lines while the copy for timed writings will increase. You will begin to spend a much larger portion of your practice time on timed writings. Use the timed writings to sustain peaks of high speed for increasing periods of time with decreasing errors. The average typist will make no more than one error per minute. The excellent typist commits three errors or under per five minutes. If you are making two or more errors per minute as you practice these timed writings, you may be out of control. Go back several lessons and review by slowing down to the stroke level, build up gradually to a level that is comfortable and controlled, and sustain it.

COMMON WORDS AND PHRASES

Flash through the easy words below.

it if is he or she if we did at our expense low cost at way
which are we are sure if their did as you see are you aware
send for the call at once within reason any other I am sure

ALTERNATING PATTERNS

very deep locker pound your cruise nature been tier pier be
and banked augment had been zucchini treatments languages I
prepared resists pleasant brought appoint appalled attended

SHIFT KEY

Muskogee, Oklahoma: Paris, France: Atlanta, Georgia; Dallas
Texas; Lansing, Michigan; Los Angeles, California; New York
Helena, Montana, Cheyenne, Wyoming, Salt Lake City, Utah NJ

REACHES

hastily therapy utilized specialized realized equalize file
excessive excitement recognized absolved acquired abject by
transcribe illustrate loyalty robot obvious participant box

HIGH-RISK COMBINATIONS

b/n
urban bank husband banner band banquet stubborn banana base
basement ban bacon bang bean number banish banker been bane
behind burdens numbs balance benefit sensible snobs obtains

Complete the error correction drill for all sections above. Following the error correction drill repeat the errored lines, typing them without error this time.

CHECKUP: Are you reading through your text before keying it? Are you very carefully proofreading your text after keying it?

PARAGRAPH PRACTICE

Type each paragraph below through twice. Complete the error correction drill between each typing.

Do not worry about errors when driving for speed, but you must not lose control and make excessive errors. When you are making excessive errors you are giving your fingers the wrong training! Wrong habits are hard to break. If out of control, take the steps to regain it.

On a daily basis women and men who work in business offices are required to be consistent and productive. To do this you must be able to work on difficult tasks for long periods of time with speed and accuracy. Learning to typewrite for long periods of time with speed and accuracy is an excellent way to prepare for the rigors of the business world.

ACCURACY SPEED ACCURACY

```
True strength lies in its daring to be gentle.          (9)
The largest accomplishment starts with the first effort.   (11)
The bond between a mother and child is a strong one.    (10)
          2       4       6       8      10      12
```

TIMED WRITINGS

There are two, five-minute timed writings below. Take three, one-minute timed writings on timed writing #1. Push for speed. Then take three to five (but not less than three), five-minute timed writings on timed writing #1. After each timing complete the error correction drill. Repeat this process on timed writing #2. Practice the preview lines before each timed writing.

Speed Range: 20 to 30+
Error Range: 3 to 5

TIMED WRITING #1

PREVIEW

```
meaningful understand objectives evaluation critical    (11)
keyboarding random concentration posture development    (22)
elements machine maximum downward you                   (29)
```

```
Your practice will be more meaningful if you understand what   (31)
you are working on when you are doing a drill. Just as it is    (42)
important to pay attention to a drill's objectives and to its  (53)
patterns, it is also important to know what you need to work on. (65)
Self-evaluation is critical to building your keyboarding       (76)
skill. Are you making errors because of your fingering, your   (88)
rhythm, your lack of concentration, or your posture? Avoid     (100)
```

random practice; it will only promote random development.   (111)
    Among the most important elements of good practice is   (122)
keeping your eyes on the copy. Place your copy at an angle to (134)
the right of your machine between 12 and 14 inches from your   (146)
eyes. Adjust the angle for maximum comfort.   (154)
    Keystroking is another very important element of good   (165)
typing. Use a downward motion when striking the keys. Move your (177)
finger quickly towards the palm to the center of the key. Far (189)
too often students will use good practice habits for a short   (201)
time only to return to bad ones. It requires dedication and   (212)
hard work to form and maintain good typing habits!   (222)
        2   4   6   8   10   12

TIMED WRITING #2

PREVIEW

communicate dictionary thoughts considered self-concept   (11)
yourself characteristic decided experiences environment   (22)
important spectrum   (26)

All of us wish to communicate well. We know that to get along (37)
well with others in the home or in the work place we need good (49)
communication skills. The dictionary tells us that to   (60)
communicate is to impart or make known our thoughts and ideas. (72)
It is not that simple though. People who communicate well have (84)
considered some of the ideas below.   (90)
    Did you know that self-concept--the way that you see   (100)
yourself-- affects the way you communicate? You have been   (111)
forming ideas about yourself since you were a baby. Every   (122)
characteristic you think you have (or do not have) goes into (134)
making up your self-concept. You have decided these things   (145)
about yourself based on your experiences and your environment. (157)
You see yourself largely based on the way important people in (169)
your life see you. How do you see yourself? Are you a winner? Or (181)
a loser? You may wonder what all of this has to do with your (192)
ability to communicate well. Your self-concept affects the   (203)
words you use, your tone of voice, what you say about yourself (215)
to others, what you say about others, and what you say to   (226)
others.   (228)
    At one extreme of the spectrum is the person who is always (240)
saying "I can't, I wish I could, but." These naysayers are   (251)
classic examples of people with negative self-concepts. At the (263)
opposite end you find those who are willing to try something (275)
new and believe they can be successful. Most of us have   (286)
positive self-concepts in some areas and negative ones in   (297)
other areas. It is important for you to recognize these areas. (309)
If you are to communicate well you must first understand   (320)
yourself.   (322)
        2   4   6   8   10   12

If you have not yet reached the minimum speed ranges and are making more than the maximum number of errors, DO NOT WORRY. Some people acquire the skill more slowly than others. Continue to practice diligently using proper technique until you master the material. It is much like losing weight. Some people can take five pounds off in a flash while others must work and work to accomplish the very same weight loss goal. But when they stick to it, they do. The final result is that they too have lost the five unwanted pounds. Stick to it and you will see; you too will obtain the speed and error range of your objectives. Dedication is the trait that distinguishes the successful.

On the other hand you may have already surpassed these goals. That is great. Continue to push for new heights as you zip through the lessons to come. Beware: Do not stop short of realizing your full potential!

Practice the lines in Part Two until you have mastered them. To continue working on your speed and accuracy go on to the second book in this series, *Shortcuts to Increase Your Typing Speed.*

About the Author

Elza Dinwiddie-Boyd has taught typewriting for the Detroit Board of Education, Wayne County Community College, and the American Business Institute in New York City. A writer and editor, she is the coauthor of *Test Without Trauma* as well as several books in the Practical Handbook Series including *Shortcuts to Increase Your Typing Speed* and *Word Processing for Beginners*.

Start building your future today with the *Practical Handbook Series* from Perigee—just call us toll-free at 1-800-631-8571, or fill out the coupon below and send your order to:

The Putnam Publishing Group
390 Murray Hill Parkway, Dept. B
East Rutherford, NJ 07073

The *Practical Handbook Series* is also available at your local bookstore or wherever paperbacks are sold.

			PRICE	
			U.S.	CANADA
_____	**Typing for Beginners**	399-51147-4	**$7.95**	**$10.50**
_____	**Touch Typing in Ten Lessons**	399-51529-1	**7.95**	**10.50**
_____	**Shortcuts to Increase Your Typing Speed**	399-51489-9	**7.95**	**10.50**
_____	**The Art of Letter Writing**	399-51174-1	**6.95**	**9.25**
_____	**Successful Business Writing**	399-51146-6	**7.95**	**10.50**
_____	**Successful Oral and Written Presentations**	399-51330-2	**6.95**	**9.25**
_____	**Job Résumés**	399-50822-8	**7.95**	**10.50**
_____	**How to Write Your First Professional Résumé**	399-51240-3	**7.95**	**10.50**
_____	**Success Through Better Memory**	399-51577-1	**7.95**	**10.50**
_____	**How to Change Careers**	399-51608-5	**7.95**	**10.50**
_____	**Word Processing for Beginners**	399-51652-2	**7.95**	**10.50**

Subtotal $_____

*Postage & Handling: $1.00 for 1 book, $.25 for each additional book up to a maximum of $3.50

*Postage & Handling $_____

Sales Tax
(CA, NJ, NY, PA) $_____

Total Amount Due $_____
Payable in U.S. Funds
(No cash orders accepted)

_____

Please send me the titles I've checked above. Enclosed is my
☐ check   ☐ money order
Please charge my
☐ Visa   ☐ MasterCard   ☐ American Express

Card #_____ Expiration Date_____

Signature as on charge card _____

Name_____

Address_____

City_____ State _____ Zip _____

Please allow six weeks for delivery. Prices are subject to change without notice.